WITHIN THIS TREE OF BONES

The Poiema Poetry Series

Poems are windows into worlds; windows into beauty, goodness, and truth; windows into understandings that won't twist themselves into tidy dogmatic statements; windows into experiences. We can do more than merely peer into such windows; with a little effort we can fling open the casements, and leap over the sills into the heart of these worlds. We are also led into familiar places of hurt, confusion, and disappointment, but we arrive in the poet's company. Poetry is a partnership between poet and reader, seeking together to gain something of value—to get at something important.

Ephesians 2:10 says, "We are God's workmanship . . ." *poiema* in Greek— the thing that has been made, the masterpiece, the poem. The Poiema Poetry Series presents the work of gifted poets who take Christian faith seriously, and demonstrate in whose image we have been made through their creativity and craftsmanship.

These poets are recent participants in the ancient tradition of David, Asaph, Isaiah, and John the Revelator. The thread can be followed through the centuries—through the diverse poetic visions of Dante, Bernard of Clairvaux, Donne, Herbert, Milton, Hopkins, Eliot, R.S. Thomas, and Denise Levertov—down to the poet whose work is in your hand. With the selection of this volume you are entering this enduring tradition, and as a reader contributing to it.

—D.S. Martin
Series Editor

Collections in this series include:

Six Sundays toward a Seventh by Sydney Lea
Epitaphs for the Journey by Paul Mariani
Within This Tree of Bones by Robert Siegel
Particular Sandals by Julie L. Moore (forthcoming)

Within This Tree of Bones

New and Selected Poems

ROBERT SIEGEL

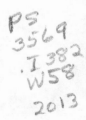 CASCADE *Books* · Eugene, Oregon

WITHIN THIS TREE OF BONES

Copyright © 2013 Robert Siegel. All rights reserved. Except for brief quotations in
critical publications or reviews, no part of this book may be reproduced in any man-
ner without prior written permission from the publisher. Write: Permissions, Wipf
and Stock Publishers, 199 W. 8th Ave., Suite 3, Eugene, OR 97401.

Cascade Books
An Imprint of Wipf and Stock Publishers
199 W. 8th Ave., Suite 3
Eugene, OR 97401

www.wipfandstock.com

ISBN 13: 978-1-62032-631-2

Cataloging-in-Publication data:

Siegel, Robert.

Within this tree of bones / Robert Siegel.

xii + 180 p.; 23 cm

ISBN 13: 978-1-62032-631-2

1. Poetry. 2. Christian Poetry. American. I. Title.

PS3553.A2 S45 2013

Manufactured in the USA.

For Julianna, Alexy,

Patrick, and Max

Contents

II. Until all Shapes are Shining

Acknowledgments

The Atlantic: Air Field (as Hanscom Air Field)

Poetry: A Bear, Ego, A Lady Who Lov'd a Swine, Hog Heaven, Them

Prairie Schooner: Christmas Eve, Peonies, Fireworks, In a Farmhouse Near Porlock, Barney Bodkin

Sewanee Review: Connection

The Cream City Review: Swimming Snake, Mussel, Slug

Midwest Quarterly: Simple Simon

V*erse:* Tiger

Books & Culture: Going On, Daddy Longlegs, The Serpent Speaks

Granite: Hunting in Widener Library, Voice of Many Waters

Midland Review: The Snow Falls, Grendel (as Sasquatch)

Image: Evening Wolves, Rat, Snail, Seer

Cresset: Deer Tick, The Surgeon After Hours, The Newly Dead, Wings (as Raphael)

Sow's Ear: Lobo

The Humanist: Great Murderers, Sheep at Nightfall (as Sheep)

The Johns Hopkins Magazine: For the technical information and phrasing in "Chaos Theory: The Lorenz Mask"

First Things: Spider

Christianity and Literature: Post-Tribulational Rapture, Chaos Theory: The Lorenz Mask

America : The Rock, Easy Rider, Aubade (as Morning Song)

The Christian Century: Giant Panda, Light Registers (as Straight at the Blue)

Arts & Letters: Mole, Mussel

For the Time Being: Matins, Morning's at Seven

The Chicago Tribune Magazine: Gettysburg: The Wheatfield

Motiv: Spinning

Your Own Poets: The Shroud

Made for Each Other: A Song of Praises,

The Tongue of the Crow: A Wisconsin Review Anthology: The Hunter

Stories for the Christian Year: A Colt, the Foal of an Ass, Blackbird in the Chimney

Poems for a Small Planet: Contemporary American Nature Poetry: Silverfish, Slug

Contemporary Poetry of New England: Looking for Mount Monadnock, Walden Communion (as Walden Once More)

The majority of these poems have also appeared in earlier books, *The Beasts & the Elders, In A Pig's Eye, The Waters Under the Earth*, and *A Pentecost of Finches: New and Selected Poems.*

I. To Dream in that Fecund Darkness

Matins

It is morning. A finch startles
the maple leaves. Everything's clear
in this first light before all thins
to a locust harping on the heat.

While day clutches at my pulse
to inject the usual anesthetic,
now, Christ, stimulate my heart,
transfuse your blood to fortify my own.

Let no light upon these sheets
diminish, Lord, before I feel you
burst inward like a finch
to nest and sing within this tree of bones.

Annunciation Over Lake Michigan

Below us Lake Michigan is another sky,
a deep, fathomless blue
that clouds of ice drift across. Our plane
slips down its glide path. Gold
blocks of light, falling in port windows,
illumine the cabin like the face
of Fra Angelico in the airline magazine.
He holds a candle to San Marco's wall
where his Virgin receives the descending Spirit—
the full spectrum flashing from the angel's wings—
while light streams in our windows, sliding
across pale faces and a blaze of turquoise seats.

Seatback up, buckled in, each rider,
cloistered in his thoughts, descends
toward clouds that rise like *putti* around us,
their harps drowned in a howl of engines.
The landing gear locks in place. Now
we shudder down the air's rough road. Soon
dark clouds receive us into thick
fog and drizzle, pressing against our windows,
before it opens to reveal the dim city
and stoplights' red reflections on wet streets.
We bump on concrete—once, twice—air brakes
roar and pitch us forward as they slow.
Stopped. The sign goes off. We unbuckle
and once more wait
to drag our heavy luggage over the earth.

Grendel

Old familiar, breathing through a reed
under the green fen,
lurker from a watery cave where flames die,
hissing your name,
Feond, Ferly, Marsh-stalker,

How often have we filed tooth and nail, shaved
a witch-knotted pelt,
only to find your fangs glittering over
a moonscape of self.

You cling, an overcoat, a cape, a Frankenstein's
monster, forsworn,
hunched moon we bring all our children,
born and unborn,

from that Transylvania of the soul where
Dracula's not dead.
Though a stake's hammered through, his heart
twitches at the crossroad,

while a fool flush with victory pauses where
weird sisters sing
what a little thing it is to kill
the anointed king.

When the full moon draws a chalk circle,
your lingering howl
floats from the burning mead hall. We follow
an uncertain trail

of dribble from your severed arm, avoid
each other's eye,
not knowing which will enter the stinking pool,
face your drooling dam,

and bring up your head that stares witless
from the whites of its eyes,
its ears stone to the voice in the reeds
murmuring prophecies

of the undying dragon and unending wars.

Swimming Snake

Climbing out of the lake,
  I first notice him
on the other side of the pier,
  swimming, his elegant head
and eye on a level with mine.

Yellow and dark green stripes
  rise to a flittering red
tongue where he glides easily
  as a thought over water
toward the tall pickerel weeds.

Each striped blade mirrors
  his long inquiring neck
while, free of the dust at last,
  at his ancient altitude,
he swims, tasting the air

with the red fire of his tongue.
  The frogs have all submerged,
leaving the burning lake
  a blank page of light
for his brilliant, flowing script—

for the elusive subtleties
  of his complicated tale
and dazzling nemesis.
  Drying off on the dock,
I smell the lake on my skin,

an odor that insinuates
  his dark evolving thesis,
his rolling, eloquent S
  that shrinks on the floor of light
to lose itself in the shadows
  of the striped pickerel weeds.

Deer Tick

No larger than a period I scramble
among the sequoia of your armhairs
unable to decide in this vast wilderness
where to drill for the life-giving well
the water of life, the warm blood.
For I am sick unto death: in my abdomen

the spirochete turns its deadly corkscrew
which I must shortly confess to the stream
pulsing from your dark red heart,
setting at liberty this ghostly germ
large in the deer's glazed eye
and the mouse's tremble.

I have carried it for generations
like a secret so long in the family
no one remembers where it came from,
like a small hiatus in the genetic code,
or a choice, an act, a curse
set loose in the wilderness of youth:

a prodigal gone to a foreign city to prosper
and return with mercenaries and fire.
I carry this secret like the memory of war,
of an evaporated nation, of a people
turned to haze on the horizon
that recedes as you drive toward it, an elusive

virus that lies dormant
and then imitates every other plague
as it maneuvers toward the final crisis:
This mist at the corner of your eye,
this telltale shape that one day will fall
over your shoulder into the morning mirror.

This voice that comes in the pit of night,
when all the others are still,
and tells you precisely what you fear,
what you cannot shrug off, repeating itself
on an endless loop:
Yes, let me tell you, I will tell you gladly.
Here, I'll put my mouth closer,
so close I won't need to whisper.

Blackbird in the Chimney

Good Friday

We hear his feet scrabble against the sheet metal,
trying for an impossible foothold. The wings
beat and beat uselessly in the liner pipe
that tapers toward the top. What intricate
dark way did he find down into this crevice
looking for a place to nest? Some strange

instinct led him under the metal flange
around the chimney top where his kind pause
to chatter every spring before heading on
like punctuation scattered to the clouds
floating in a long sentence across March.
He's trapped for sure. Sometimes one or two

will fluster down the main pipe. At the bottom
when the damper opens, the sooty pair
will squawk and whirr into the light,
true to the old saw, *The way up is down,*
lucky their hell has a convenient exit.
But his is sealed—the only way out is up.

I unscrew the metal chimney top and search
with a flashlight a crevice twenty feet deep.
The pipe curves: I cannot see the bottom.
Meanwhile his every feather's and claw's slightest
twitch is magnified by the metal liner.
"He's here. He's right here. I can hear him"—

my daughter's voice comes up from the fireplace,
shaking at his proximity, delicate as his bones.
"It's only a bird," I call down to her. "It doesn't suffer—
not the way we would suffer. A bird can't think

that it *has* suffered—*is* suffering—*will* suffer."
So ends my conjugation, muffled in the pipe.
Still—he suffers," she says, and for a moment
the bird is still. Then the earnest scrabbling begins
once more. I lower a triple hook on fishing line
again and again. No luck. But my doing something
helps her and helps me too on that windy roof,
one step from rotten gutters. Once, I see the gleam

of an eye and imagine I've got him. For two days
I climb up and down the ladder with ever more
elaborate schemes until the scratching stops
and I must tell her at last nothing will work.
"Two days"—the Humane Society says on the phone—
"A third and, believe me, it's finished for sure."

My daughter is growing up. She understands.
She doesn't want her father to take more risks.
Her silence matches mine now, holding, as it does,
the neighbor drowned in a river, the classmate dying
of leukemia, the jogger struck down quadriplegic.
Her dad couldn't help this time, unlike the time

he drilled through the kitchen wall at 1 a.m.
behind the refrigerator to make an exit
for the shy and unwilling-to-be-rescued
hamster, who finally came out for cheese
and her maternal wheedling. Or the time
he released the gerbil from the cooled-off furnace

after listening for his scratching on the pipes.
That one died of old age in his sleep,
a seer, having passed on (if gerbils can)
a vision to his cagemate of a cold
dark place at the bottom, an inedible wall,
hunger, thirst, and fear—when, suddenly,
beyond all expectation, the wall opened
and light came through and a warm human hand.

The Newly Dead

Time is the moving shadow of eternity.
—Blake

The newly dead are concerned
they can't help us. It was only
a moment ago they were trying to clear up
some ultimate point, some elusive light.

They leave us with the other dust,
are gone, and we are here. Where?
Perhaps it's we who leave while they,
caught for a moment in a puzzling reverie,

wake immersed in the full light
knowing themselves and the place at last,
to find we have plunged ahead in time,
shadowy creatures chasing the shadow of a shadow.

The Surgeon After Hours

Strange how they visit me at 3 a.m.,
  some accusing, some grateful, some both—
faces tight with pain, flushed and heavy, or
  indifferent, anesthetized. They take shape
like patches of fog in my headlights while I
  thread these dark streets home. They come
beseeching, pleading with me, though I can
  no longer help them, nor tell them not to come,
or rise transcendent with resignation as if they know
  something I don't—I, the technician hired
to postpone the inevitable. They rise
  like this one, the woman whose heart
stopped under the knife for seven minutes.
  Later, she said she'd died and seen a peculiar light.
I don't recall her words, only her face
  when she tried to say just what it was she saw—
that and the way her hand, birdlike,
  flew over the bedclothes. I wonder,
do our brain cells at the edge
  burst with a final energy? Is the last
illusion more real than life? I don't know:
  hallucination won't explain it, explains
nothing, really. The divisible flesh both is
  and isn't us—this much I feel and more:
we are the whole left when the parts are gone.
  Something surrounds us
we have to lose everything else to find.

Light Registers

Her spine straightens by an inch.
Someone coughs, goes out of the room.
They pray again. Three days later
her shoulders lose their narrow pinch.

They pray every day for an hour:
one leg has lengthened, a knee bends.
Soon light registers and her voice box
limbers. A slow power

burns through her parents' hands. They,
father and mother, can hardly believe,
but the ministry of their hands murmurs
through the mouths of neighbors. Later

when she is whole, they claim
one closer to her than themselves has done
again what he did—but the world will not
notice, in the fall-out of news, his name

anymore than usual. Who can explain these hours
to legions of the reasonable and decent?
All we know is the healing love
of one tending her atoms like flowers.

Yet none can deny that the healed girl—
despite our offended unbelief—
opens her eyes, smiles straight at the blue china
floating toward her rich with cream and cereal.

for Francis MacNutt

God's Back

I will cover you with my hand until I have
passed by; then I will take away my hand
and you shall see my back. —Exodus

Beginning with C in the dank school basement,
You taught me to hold a note on the silver trombone
With the dented gold bell. Out the window, grass
Rioted in the humid air. An occasional breeze
Brought its green smell past the scratched upright
Piano where you patiently struck C—

Your finger pointing to that simple law
While my horn wandered and bellowed
Like a golden calf after the silage of Egypt.
Breaking an aspirin tablet in two, you swallowed,
Struck the note again—
Nodding for emphasis while drops of sweat flashed

Falling from your eyebrows to the keys.
My second note likewise flattened, strayed
While on the wall above us musical deities frowned
In a pantheon containing the marble pallors
Of Handel, Mozart, Bach—promising no manna
To me, lost in a wilderness of sounds.

Miraculously I hung on for a season
As first trombone, slid back to second,
After another winter quit the band
To mouth notes silently in the all-school chorus.
Feeling guilty and relieved, I watched
The back of your shirt soak through with sweat

While you wrestled music from the air
Over the dwindling remnant of the faithful.
Now, hearing of your heart attack, I recall
How your hand described an elegant B
With a forceful downstroke and two loops
As we stalled and wambled through a waltz,

And that day, pale, you handed down scores
You'd spent the night transposing. Even at twelve
I sensed our brazen wails and tinkling cymbals
Didn't deserve such sacrifice. Whatever
Mountain it was you faithfully ascended
Its god was overwhelming, the music of his progress,

The single note you heard as he passed by,
Struck you deaf to our tinhorn blasphemies—
Even as I guessed, when you played the Ninth
Symphony on the old, scratched 78s,
How it must have deafened Beethoven
To hear the divine tread fall again and again.

for Harold Brunt

Fireworks

A few reports at midnight the night before
opened spaces in the sky and in my sleep,
and by the early morning of the Fourth
the bittersweet smell was lurking in the air.
For weeks I'd stared at mauve, green,
and red rice paper packets of firecrackers
covered with mystical Chinese characters,
contraband I'd saved for all that winter—
round cherry bombs, bottle rockets,
whizzbangs, Roman candles, ladyfingers,
shipped in a plain brown cardboard box.

Behind Dick Leckband's house that afternoon
we blew up toy entrenchments, bushes, crabgrass,
whole strings dissolving, drifting down in flakes,
cans rocketing through the air over cannoncrackers,
rattling windows until a cruiser idled by,
its red light flashing like a Roman candle.

At dusk with cousins, aunts, and uncles,
we hurried to the park and the town's display,
spreading blankets in the growing dark,
waiting forever, dizzy with yearning, until
unannounced, except for a fizz of sparks,
a solo rocket cracked open the heavens.

Sighing together in a wave, we watched
pure silver scrawl across the sky, golden rain,
green crowns of light and red Ezekiel's wheels,
purple cataracts, orange asters, yellow fountains—

the whole earth blooming in the heavens
again and again and again while we gazed up
from the dark void at fire spreading out
in a recurring pattern each time different:
the secret work of gravity and light
by which everything came suddenly out of nothing,
fading back into it, rising and falling,
until the end when the American flag
unfurled and blazed brilliantly on its wire
down to a coal, leaving a sweet haze
we walked home through in the double dark
among the crowds murmuring like leaves.
Eyes, ears sated, too tired almost to move,
we stumbled beside our parents who were lost
in talk of ordinary things as if they hadn't
just seen the worlds created and expire.

Drunk on the lingering smoke and its fled music,
hot and sticky, we climbed upstairs
to the sheets glowing in the white summer night
where, scarcely out of our clothes, we fell asleep
to dream in that fecund darkness of the light,
the beginning and end and all things in between.

for Richard Leckband, 1940–2002

The Serpent Speaks

> *Soul: Look on that fire, salvation walks within.*
> *Heart: What theme had Homer but original sin?*
> > *—Yeats*
>
> *And three begot the ten thousand things.*
> > *—Lao Tzu*

I am another vine
in the great democracy of vines
part of the complexity that defies explanation
part of the tree you put your back to,
alert, but never suspecting.
I am the cold coil around the warm trunk,
I expand
as your lungs, poor rabbits, twitch and swell.
I am a long story with lovely yellows
        and dapples and shades
a beginning, middle, and end that you can get lost in
a sunny patch followed by a shadow
a green dapple and twist, the turn, the unexpected
        reversal.
When you come to the denouement
                and my tail narrows to nothing
you wish to go back to the beginning and start over
where the red lie flickers in the leaves
beneath eyes like mica moons.

It is the old story, the beginning of everything
but really a long divagation and excursus
in which the woman naked and trembling
        complains to the man, weeping over and over
                and his voice rises in sharp jabs
                        while all their unborn children listen.
It is something that interrupts the afternoon, the first day,

and history begins and wanders off for millenia
   missing the whole point.
It is these subtle shades on my scales
this maze of intricate lines
that lead back upon themselves in endless recursions
that fascinate you, that lead you endlessly
from my tail into my mouth.
In the moving light of the jungle I am a simple
body-stocking of shadows and weave
under a fritillary of bird cries to a sensuous music
a harmony to all your doings
promising you the ultimate knowledge in my belly
down the dark tube of years:
Light and shadow, light and shadow, the days and nights pass
with increasing speed like stations and their intervals
and you sway holding the strap
the car-lights flickering
wondering whatever was your original destination.

When fiction held out its red lie among the roses
you followed it down my dark throat.
It seemed utterly reasonable. Then you were Methuselah
carrying each of his 900 years like a brick on his back
Abraham's wild surmise with a knife
Joseph starving in a hole
and Moses singeing his feet in the wilderness.
Next they hung you from two sticks and slowly
everything grew more dramatic:
Augustine heard the children in the garden
Aquinas fled from the naked peasant
and Columbus woke in a sweat, the voices still singing
of a lost world
of amber waves and alabaster
until Lord Amherst gave his blankets to the Indians
Franklin saw the flashing key
and Washington sold his horse for pasturage
until the utterly reasonable Robespierre offered up his head
Lenin popped from a boxcar

and Einstein gave you the terrible secret
which I had promised,
a man of violins and God.
Now the story has gotten out of hand
as you swarm upon yourselves like maggots
    on a diminishing dung-pile
        and frenzied, move toward the catastrophe
history a string of boxcars
    each a century stuffed to overflowing
        until the last leaps the track.

Meanwhile I who am the truth move
scintillatingly, with grace in my own shadow
telling the story: *There was a man, and a woman. . .*
and the sun rose
        and they went on a long journey
and night fell and they did not know where they were.

Such is knowledge, such is the fruit I offered
    without the encumbrances of love, without listening
        without the tree of fire that burns
below all movement, all shining, the tree below the bones
whose flames reach through the skeleton and hover
just over the fingers
        and burn away the forest where the ego
goes crying, alone—one eye balancing the other
bilaterally symmetrical—
of what it has and what it hasn't
until all shapes are shining and
fear falls away shriveling like a black net
    and the wisdom of God dances freely before you
and the glowing fruit blushes for the mouth.

I see all clearly and can tell you
the end of things, knowing you will not listen,
for my knowledge is cold here in the forest
and you will follow the shifting arabesque
        of moonlight on my mica-glint, my scales

moving like the sequins of days, events,
    the rise of stocks and the next presidential election
            and the price of wheat futures in a drought.
So I go on, flowing into my own shape
into the darkness I have made, subservient
(and this is the bitterness beyond all blankness)
at the last to another purpose
    which you cannot guess, which rings in these leaves
like the harps and fiddles of insects too high
for your range of hearing—a music which drives me
into the narrowing circle I have made
tail in mouth, swallowing until
                        I vanish
and everything in this circle vanishes with me.

Great Murderers

What man can pass judgment
on all the good and evil you have done?
—Mao Tse-tung

Great murderers sleep well,
who murder civilly, pursuing peace.
Millions gone under desert ground
are indistiguishably wheat

nodding over radish-cheeked children.
A thousand rice paddies push over them
spring shoots in a green haze:
The dead are adjusting to pleasant ways,

as, indeed, why should they not? Their killers
wear simple clothes, meet no visible ghosts,
assume for the press avuncular smiles
soft as flour ground from the host

of reformed fathers. In age, the plow of care
sows sparingly a few white hairs
like flowers at their temples. Their good
talk and simple manners to the multitude

are loaves and fishes. They miss no sleep,
nor does their hand sere with the yellow leaf
as, kindly, to widow and fatherless they hold up
cold water in a cup.

In the Cosmetic Lab: Rabbit #234

Red-eyed, white hair
teased by generations
of breeding for Easter,
he crouches

in a prayer posture
over a steel grid
with fifty of his kind.
He makes no sound

but the slow burning
rasp of his breath.
His long ears flop
over like broken lilies,

their shadow his
only privacy
for pain. Acid
has burned

away the fur from one
whole side. Now the skin,
shriveled orange, exposes
ribs and pink

rosefields of lungs. The acid
tested will be
present in minute amounts
in facial cream.

My beautiful lady,
the next time you rub it in
ask the mirror: What is
softer than your skin?

The Disconsolate Chimera

The loud lament of the disconsolate chimera.
—T. S. Eliot

The disconsolate chimera wandered the waste
where the fasting figure refused to take much notice,
though the dreaming monster offered him a taste
of a perfect loaf of bread. And then—it boasted—

kingdoms and empires of the world, total power
to run everything. But the figure answered no.
            And last, at the apex of the trial's hour,
the spiritual strength to bend all things below

to his own will. But the figure looked away,
and the chimera, gathering up its wavering folds
of diaphanous mirage, floated into the sky,
where loud as a thousand banshees its vanishing cry
failed to frighten the figure bowed below,
grieving for all who'd perish on this way.

Air Field

All day the great planes gingerly descend
an invisible staircase, holding up
their skirts and dignity like great ladies
in technicolor histories, or reascend,
their noses needling upward like a compass
into a wild blue vacuum,
leaving everything in confusion behind:

In some such self-deceiving light as this
we'll view the air force base when moved away
from where its sleepless eye revolves all night.
We'll smile and recollect it conversationally—
tell with what ease the silver planes dropped down
or how they, weightless, rose above
our roof. We'll pass it with the sugar and cream,

forever sheltered from this moment's sick
surprise that we have lived with terror, with pride,
the wounded god circling the globe, never resting,
that in the morning and the evening we have heard
his cry, have seen him drag his silver wings
whining with anguish like a huge
fly seeking to lay its deadly eggs.

for Robert Lowell

Stalker

All things betray thee, who betrayest Me.
—Francis Thompson

I hand my kids their lunches at the door.
You loiter in the silences they leave,
till I shut you out by turning on the news,
its snap and crackle my after-breakfast fix,
anodyne to the Monday morning blues—
a lurking shadow, easily ignored

and forgotten. But only an hour later
a hand waves at me, spinning in the washer,
and clutches inside my chest as a small bird
bounces off the window and the freezer
drops a cube. Afraid of coming unstrung,
I take something to pull myself together

and sit down with the paper: *New York City
Close to Bankruptcy Second Time This Year.
Uneasy Truce in Middle East Follows
Surprise Assault. Publicity Seeker
Sentenced to Life. More Toxic Chemicals
Found Infiltrating Our Air and Water.*

I throw it down, wishing the kids home early,
their greedy hands, the yammering trapeze
of small wants and hurts. Your soapy voice
slides toward me, foaming from the TV.
I call my neighbor. Drunk, she confesses
marriage is costing her her sanity. . .

Is that you cutting through the screen?
A darkness circles in me, wanting out,
like ice circling the bottom of my glass.

The doorbell grieves and grieves, but I ignore it,
yet lie here listening to the walls whisper
your desire. Sunlight crumbles bit by bit.

I get up to draw the drapes. The doorknob
appears to turn, yet the door stays shut.
You murmur you want all of me
And what I hold most dear . . . . Still not enough—
you want every last thing. My God, you!
whom I once with one little finger could fend off.

Barney Bodkin

Barney Bodkin broke his nose,
Without feet we can't have toes;
Crazy folks are always mad,
Want of money makes me sad.

[for Sabina, in a state ward for the senile]

"It's Barney Bodkin holds us in,
I've often thought. He looks so queer
with his nose like a great eggplant,
the stethoscope hooked to each ear,

as if he's trying to figure where
that last bit of life is raising hell
on its little drum. In this hospital
I've noticed, to be ill is to be well:

For those who lift their chins over
the rail and pule and cry
for their teeth, are let down
by a white hand—sometimes tied

and spoonfed a sugary poison.
Ach! I got wise the first week,
saw the lively wheeled to the inner ward,
the still ones washed out with the sheets.

Now from this crib I watch herself
who brings me food on a steel plate
to see if she has the password: her eyes
go blank like the *Cream o' Wheat*.

Then Barney comes thumping and squeezing
and listening, trying to catch the little seed
that tickles in one ear and out the other,
running loose among the patients, who need

quiet he says—the quiet he carries
boxed in his cabbagey hand, nodding
like a tomato plant, listening
to where the earth down deep is dead.

Oh, I pretend to be asleep or too dim
to notice his fingers brush over me, nor yet
his cold root pinching my arm,
his breath about my head like African violets.

I am better than he thinks, my sheets are clean,
mornings I count my toes twice over,
checking out both eyes, and know
they'll get the message to me wherever.

And some blue-bulbed night
after Bodkin has scraped past here
with that tiffley long vegetable breath of his,
I will inch over the bars,

slip out of this disguise they put me in,
and squeeze through that window
toward the river
where the others are holding up the stars."

Them

There are men in the village of Erith
Whom nobody seeth or heareth . . .
—from a traditional limerick

On the shore of the river where you picnic,
a part of the day is missing
that was there in your bright predictions,
a blank like the sand in your sandwich

that can't be gotten rid of, though you try
shifting your seat. At the office
the paper crawling under your pencil
is significantly silent about them.

In class when someone writes on the blackboard
these leave a slight chalky aura
that fades when the bell rings. You wonder
what it was they were going to make clear.

At home they play cribbage in the parlor
silently advancing the pegs
while you in the kitchen have forgotten
the salami and rye you came out for.

Walking out, you sense them already
before you around the corner,
find their fingerprints on the window,
their breath rising over the shingles.

At last, though you've no wish to see them,
you find you cannot live without them,
for, foul-breathed, dark with loose threads,
or radiant, eaten by light,
one will, one day, lift a hand
and the map on his hand will match yours.

Sheep at Nightfall

They are foam collecting
    on the shore of the field.
Backs yellow with dust
    they lean against the gate;
now one, now another lifts a voice
    vibrating and torn as the Irish.

They are richly dressed, each wigged
    like a British justice. Yet
they move together like slaves
    bent under Pharaoh,
to be folded into the dark
    eating every green thing
and complaining at the dust of their daily bread.

If March shows the icy
    back of his robe,
they will go no further.
    Eyes thick with rheum,
they feel death's finger shake the ground:
    Thousands in one night
rot where they fall like patches of late snow.

Still the old ram carries his head
    like the treasure of Persia,
uttering a melodious question,
    knowing he will be answered
when the sun comes striding
    from the oratorio of the hills,
touching his fleece with gold.

Simple Simon

Now he wags his head, now beats the floor,
Out of time with all the dignity,
Pomp, and music in this service of our Lord,
This tread and pause of elders steady as trees.

Constrained inside his head all leaps and pushes
To a blur of light, to a hugger-mugger joy,
As if a wind would take each hand and rush
Him birdlike to the altar with a cry.

We see his ungainly shadow, not
What his soul by its sharp hunger proves—
That we are fickle with our faculties
And by our spastic wills evade our love—

Unlike this simple child whose spirit easily
Outstrips where angels groan and dare not.

Christmas Eve

While cattle stupidly stare
over straw damp from their breathing
and the horse lazily stirs
over his trough, and the lantern
licks at shadows in corners,

in the woods the wild ones gather,
the rabbit twitching with care,
sooty shrew, and imperial mole
with the hands of a lost politician,
to shine in the branch-broken light

of a moon which in mid-career
lights up a church of snow.
Now one paw after another
about the bones of weeds
in a soft worrying circle

the helpless ones dance out their fear,
watching the glittering air
where he shines in the eyes of the others
naked, with nothing to wear.
Long before he comes to the stable

to the shrew's moving smudge on the snow
to the mole's ineffectual gesture
to the soft hide of the hare
he comes, warming each creature
naked in the fangs of the year.

A Bear

A white bear groped the orchard of my dream,
Gulped cherries down his inexact raw throat,
His paws were bleeding blindly and his muzzle,
Sweet cherry, sweet cherry, sweet cherry—

                              I shot
The huge blind bear so enormously stuffing
Himself with winds of flowers, heaps of grass-
Green partridges, red and yellow marmosets,

And down he came with the bread of heaven
Thunderous on my brazen coat. I deferred
Handshakes and all grave bear solemnities,
Touching his wounded eyes and ears and nose.

He sang a slow song as he smoothly died,
Lifting his nose to the east and to the west,
A thin and quavering note for so large a beast
That crept in a slow stain across my vest.

Then blazing like a furnace of white snow
He lifted cavernous wings and drew
To his full height—his blood hung in bright beads—
He flexed his feathers once and flew

In a flattering arc to the sun that swelled
Imperceptibly to drink him in, then shone
As usual. Each day it's shone the same
Since I first rubbed my eyes to find him gone.

The Snow Falls

The snow falls with abandon, falls
every which way down. Each intricate flake
covers the scarred earth with its white coat.

How light a caress, this inch of snow:
it touches the trees, clings to the wires,
a molting of angels, a celestial worry

over all things. Now the mouse huddles
under leaves, the mole digs deeper,
the owl glides quietly, offering absolution.

The moon hangs above it, a cold query.
Sparrows circle from the chimney like ashes
while the cat peers steadily from the skeletal

shadow of the fence. In the wave's swell
a shark turns suddenly
unappeasable, a whale swallows chiliads

of krill. So the world groans and dissolves
into itself. In this darkness the thing happens:
lives become other lives, are cast up

for the moon's clear inspection, pox-faced,
wearing a dark coat and hat. Sometimes she seems
about to comment. The surf erases another line.

All this hunger and movement, this striving.
The snow throws itself down in pity
from the order of heaven where things are clear

as the horizon retreating from a space shuttle
or the edge of Africa, a calm and simple line.
From there the snow comes, an infinite army

who throw themselves down, wings and all,
in utter abandon. Each tiny hosanna
patterns the air for a moment. Each small

forgiveness lights upon the earth, dissolves.

Chaos Theory: The Lorenz Mask

Odd bicycle, twin ramshorns spiraling out,
wings of a butterfly, or a harlequin mask—
Chaos Theory graphs on the computer
as two elegant galactic spirals—a simple
formula revealing to us the pattern
of irregular faucet drippings, mosquito populations
swelling and shrinking, the tumbling of Saturn's moons,
fluctuation of heartbeats, brainwaves, stock markets,
the fall of water, or the fall of dice.

The exotic characters of its new jargon,
the *strange attractor* and *Feigenbaum numbers*,
bifurcation diagram and *fractals*,
may even help us prophesy the weather
accurately, and other unpredictables.
Numbers "sensitive to initial conditions"
will not ignore an effect "as minuscule
as the gravitational attraction
of an electron at the edge of the galaxy"—
Who was that Lorenz-masked strange attractor?

This messy new mathematics is more like nature
"than the chaste one handed down to us by Newton,"
describes creativity as "the chaotic process
that selectively amplifies small fluctuations"
until the twin galactic wings are
butterfly, cho-cho-san, papillon, psyche.

Schizophrenics are extremely sensitive
to initial conditions, float randomly
from thought to thought,
while dictators, the rigid, and obsessed
find all things take them to the strange attractor.

A butterfly trampled in a prehistoric swamp
by a time-traveler inevitably changes
the future to which the traveler returns.
Meanwhile a wing fluttering in Tahiti
conspires in a blizzard over New York City.
For want of a nail a shoe, et cetera.

Musical, artistic, literary creations,
set in motion by the choice of a first measure,
brush stroke, or word, may then flow
conditionally to their conclusions, as
Of Man's first disobedience and the fruit becomes
Through Eden took their solitary way.
Despite all Pandemonium and the nine-day trip
through Chaos by the great Antagonist,
an order evolves, comes around again
like a butterfly's wing, a raccoon's mask
or the double helix, that old dipsy-doodle.

Hunting in Widener Library

Ribithoids, by Macrowcz, 073.869.10-6A, written on a
slip of paper floating between fingers before him
to the narrow door, hedged in stone,
the same stone shelving out over,
under, eons of books compressed into
ten levels, wedged in steel vertebrae,
ganglia for the enormous brain that sheds
a little light out these windows—once
John Harvard's few shelves, now plunging
stories into the earth.

                    Going down
from Level 4 to Level 3, from American
to English literature, oppressed
by the millions of cells thinking
in the darkness between covers,
the word buried in the pulp of trees.
Down to Sub-level B. Stairs clang: up the
square mouth a soft meadowy thing in a sweater,
books pressed quivering to her, cloud
of flowers, momentary. Then that staid
smell of old authors shrinking in the cellar,
distant seed of the tree of knowledge
more elusive for its sextillion sprouts,
steady and shrewd scent of worlds
never to be cracked. Down
to Sub-level D. The slip is pale
against the blue fluorescent damp—
potable stone.

Ribithoids, by Macrowcz, an unintelligible title
by an unpronounceable author—reason enough:
This is the book to break that chain of looking up to add
to what one knows, which always leads to

looking up something else. Bald-headed man asleep on
the second, third, and eighth volumes
of Crabbits' *Dictionary of the Visigoths.* The
radiator clucks like a brooding hen

This is the book to give the secret
whole—the isolate knowledge, ethereal
and complete, in whose faintest iota swims
the luminous gnat-swarm of the worlds.
This is the fruit whose pierced skin
froths with stars, at whose succulent word
the snake swallows his tail into light.
This is the fruit of that forbidden tree
whose roots crawl over maps and faces,
sink through this cellar nine
times all of relative space to the center.

He moves along the last aisle, bulb burnt out,
lighting a match over the backward books—
Ribwort, Ribs—then nothing but solid
wall one inch away from Macrowcz 10 6A
buried in stone!

The snake's skeleton rattles through the pipes.
The gleaming-headed sleeper after knowledge
snores. Back to Coleridge and Lowes'
Road to Xanadu, where he who pauses to pluck
a footnote is lost. Back to the link
that is not missing, back to Coleridge and
opium, the regulated stall, books
to check in and books to check out.

The root goes too deep.

Post–Tribulational Rapture

> *What we're trying to do is learn*
> *something about the biochemical fate*
> *of the gold after it enters the body.*
> —*Professor Frank Shaw*

"What we're trying to do is meld
the proteins in the blood with gold,"

he said. His beakers gleamed and perked.
Not since the hunting of the quark

had I been captivated so
by science. He smiled, "Yes, I know,

it's an ancient dream of sorts,"
and paused, the bubbling of retorts

his undersong. "The dream in alchemy
was to turn lead into gold. Actually,

we want the opposite, gold to disappear
taking deposits—arthritis, that is—from here—"

he pointed to his elbow—"the joints."
So gold, this philosopher's stone, anoints

with healing till the bones are clear
and move without pain. Gone the crippling fire—

the calcium sublimed, ethereal,
shines in the dark flesh, which no longer feels

the stiffening cage of the skeleton—
rather as if the bones, risen and gone

like bars of light, vanish in the sun
while the flesh divides the air without pain.

Fun City

*(Note: This poem was written in the early 70s,
before the advent of the PC and the Internet.)*

whatever we now believe necessary
to vocalize by phone will
then as soon as we think of it
immediately communicate

        BZZZ this is a recording

we will sing through an electronic choir
that would baffle the seraphim
meanwhile in each office memo boards
will relay every effect at intervals

        I am sorry but the number

and the general intermaster
will relate on pre-established templates
the coded responses inclusive without fail
of every variable exponentially considered

        you have dialed is no longer

and the minute electric filaments
connecting every home and every brain
through the miniputer inserted at birth
between the skull and pineal gland

        in service. Will you please

light instantaneously and unite
in one vast grid of intervolved
opinion and consideration of taste
the least whim of reservation about

hang up and try again. This

the slightest readjustment necessary
to the entirely electronic government
operating interdependently and fusing
each unitary cell in its complectic brain

is a recording. I am (CLICK)

Primary Red

You are every image, and yet
I am homesick for you.
                        —Rumi

Red night of lips, of fuchsia
bowers, red pollen choking the heart.

Red of lights standing, streets blazing
soldiers melting into the ground,

Red of the sun burning down into itself.
of liquors, of lacquers, of heart's blood

pulsing through wrists and fingernails,
earlobes and nipples.

Red of high noon, and the last
thin thread of lips along the west.

Red as a dark thought on the darkest night,
red as a reflection in the dog's eye.

Red as a skirt, as the hibiscus,
as salvia, as the cloven worm.

Red as a mouth holding the only word
secret until dawn speaks.

Red as the utter penetralium
that all love knows.

Red as a lace slip, as a bikini,
as a kimono and Chinese lantern.

Red as the light speaking in two heads
together, a tongue

caressing a lip, a finger
opening a bud to a rose.

The red shaken loose by language
into the fire of contemplation.

A red star winking ,
drawing the heart to the red planet

that swims down
to drown in the blue ovum of the sea.

Red of the bull flag
and the toreador's hose.

Red of a firetruck passing in the night
and the taillights of a thousand semis,

red as a gas pump, as
the waitress' smeared lipstick,

red as this Bic pen, as a red plastic notebook.
Red as the roofs of Florence.

and the monkey's cap in the Doge's portrait.
or the pale red houses of Rome.

Red as a poem, approaching the mind,
red as a snake's tongue flickering,

slipping into the earth
under a stone,

red as the retinal glow
on the eyelid afterwards.

Red—red as feet pried
from the nail in the foot of the cross.

A Psalm of Midlife

> *. . . to live more free from outward cumber.*
> *—John Woolman's Journal*

Cumber is my lord, it's more than I want.
  It makes me carry in from the minivan;
It makes me carry out to the curb;
  It distresses my soul.
It leads me in paths of acquisitiveness
  For the economy's sake.

Ach, though I walk through the valley of forgetfulness,
  I know no peace,
For cumber is with me:
  My cellphone and my iPad,
They remind me.

It prepares a caloric table before me
  In the presence of my colleague;
It has put a mortgage on my head;
  My budget overflows.
Surely lender and tax-collector shall follow me
  All the days of my life,
And I shall make monthly payments forever.

Walden Communion

The New England landscape
is like a radish salad.
—Lenaye Marsten

Comestible, comprehensible,
  heaped up in digestible portions:
Thoreau had eaten far in Concord
  and still this knoll
with its floor of puce-colored leaves
  under May's green mist
feeds the visitor. These trees
  map out silence like pins
a faintly invisible gold
  breathable, drinkable
as we bite into sharp cheddar, brown
  bread, and drink grape juice
at Walden, my daughter's
  illegal cat under my coat.

Some kind of universe turns here.
  Each new leaf is a star, a wafer,
a harvest the golden grasshopper
  above the Boston Statehouse,
the plague of tourists
  (of which we are four),
cannot devour: the pilgrims
  from the Ganges,
the agitated throttles of bikers,
  the hoarse voices that
rattle with aluminum cans,
  the lovers treasure-hunting in the bushes.

Thirty years ago there was little water,
   sixty years ago E. B. White despaired of the litter,
in Thoreau's day the trees were small,
   the train visible as it hooted and smoked to the west,
the ice cutters muffled in heavy coats, busy.

But silence has survived:
   the water is back
the litter gone
   the train invisible.
This intergalactic space between trees has survived
   all the calibrated limitations,
this silence of the wren
   whose brilliant plumage no one has yet seen,
this voice that comes up with light about it
   in perpetual astonishment from the blue-green waters
that fill the oval of the bay.

Here among the dim gray maples
   and the white paper birch
the cat scatters old leaves like cut-off wings.
   We finish the grape juice, the dark loaf.
We have not yet seen the cairn
   nor the model of the hut near the parking lot
where the Concord dump used to be,
   but, moving back through this gray
afternoon, breathing last years' leaves,
   we glance at each other—
the four of us—
   our hunger satisfied.

for L., L., & C.

Looking for Mt. Monadnock

She flowed into a foaming wave;
She stood Monadnoc's head.
—Emerson, "The Sphinx"

We see the sign "Monadnock State Park"
as it flashes by, after a mile or two

decide to go back. "We can't pass by Monadnock
without seeing it," I say, turning around.

We head down the side road—"Monadnock Realty,"
"Monadnock Pottery," "Monadnock Designs,"

but no Monadnock. Then the signs fall away—
nothing but trees and the darkening afternoon.

We don't speak, pass a clearing, and you say,
"I think I saw it, or part of it—a bald rock?"

Miles and miles more. Finally, I pull over
and we consult a map. "Monadnock's right there."

"Or just back a bit there." "But we should see it—we're
practically on top of it." And driving back

we look—trees, a flash of clearing, purple rock—
but we are, it seems, too close to see it:

It is here. We are on it. It is under us.

Universal Pan

> *while universal Pan. . .*
> *Led on th' eternal spring.*
> *—Paradise Lost, Book IV**

My beard springs in the black hedge,
its shadow my glad grief,
my tears running from the rock's foot.

My broken ribs are these ridges,
the hollow of my belly and groin,
this valley.

My fingers grope
through every root and branch.
From the lake in each palm
a sun bursts.

Thorns caught in my hair
spring to holly, laurel, roses.
My teeth are stars

in the open mouth of night,
the moon my glittering eye.
Each moment I call,

Wake! Wake! Wake!
and shake the winter's bones
in the wind's fist.

Still, you do not hear,
numb in your sleep of snow.

*Milton here suggests that Pan, the pagan
god of nature, is actually Christ, the Logos.

Oil Spill

You are in the small gray light
that wakes from the east, the shore
that outlines my day. Empty
sky is your medium. You promise

nothing to me who beach
like a ruptured supertanker
glutting the shore with oil,
slick gull, dying of surfeit.

I wade out, coated
with unctuous night.
Stones cut my feet—
my tongue crusted with sand.

Immerse me again, wash clean
the broken feather of my will.
Dry me with your wind,
massage my sluggish heart.

Then drop me from the bluff
into sharpening light,
where for hours I may climb
the thermal updraft of your breathing.

March Woodpecker

I was amazed that it could last, for
I thought that because of its littleness
it would suddenly have fallen into nothing.
             —Julian of Norwich

A red-headed downy woodpecker clings sideways
to the suet cage, rapidly swallowing seeds
embedded in the fat between bars. Again

and again his fierce appetite, quick eye, and crown
of fire snatch and snatch, and then—
gone, a wing, a flash of light. I see

blue sky stretch seamless over the whole earth,
a low green flame of grass, and feel
the sullen clay I stand on stir, a soil

hard as rock, break and mix with water,
feathers, loam, twigs, and faded leaves.
Among them, too small to see, a single cell

divides—divides again: *All shall be well.*

Going On

Once I am sure there's nothing going on
I step inside. . .
                    —*Philip Larkin, "Church Going"*

Once I am sure that something's going on
I enter, tired of mere ritual,
of liturgy where no work is done,
of punctual repetitions. One can tell
by the face and gestures of the celebrant—
or, better, by the others celebrating
this continually renewed act
of grace (invisible except where a look can't
hide the intimate and present fact).

I go forward, even though mostly summer
is sitting, damp and musty, in the pews,
to where a few in the mid-week evening glimmer
raise hands standing, while others move
to kneel where the priest lays hands on them,
often saying words better than he knows
to say. There I stay until the end
of the service—once more hear the strong love
commending me to eat that I might live.

And so I do. This church's architecture
is nothing special. There are few monuments
or memorials present here.
Only the window in the sanctuary has yet
embraced stained glass. The walls are bare.
What happens here is rarely to be discovered
in anything but the people—well- or ill-favored,
oppressed by poverty, by wealth, by having spent
themselves to no purpose. None is good,
in our first understanding of that word. All come

with a sense, dim or clear, that what they amount to fails,
the intelligence that tirelessly adds the sum
of things in a clear system, sparks, falters,
shorts out—leaving us to press the mystery
against the roof of the mouth, to hug the ghost
once fused with flesh and still enfleshed in us,
until our spirit answers *Abba* and we know
by living contact what we can't deduce.

It is in the faces, and these come and go
like the spirit, which wanders where it will.
Even Canterbury's merely a heap of stones
until the spirit enters there and wells
in living voices, and thirty bishops dance
gravely to a voice beyond the chancel's.
Let no elegy hang here like the ghost of incense.
Rather, let walls tumble, altars grow wild—new
ones will be raised up in three days (or less)
of the sort the living spirit passes through.

*Note: The dance of bishops occurred spontaneously
in Canterbury Cathedral a few years ago.*

II. Other Voices:
Until all Shapes are Shining

Inchworm

This strange disease of modern life,
with its sick hurry, its divided aims.
                   —Matthew Arnold

I never feel quite all together.
Part of me leaves before I've gotten here,
abstracted as I am by numbers
by that invisible world where one plus one equal two
by the calculus, pebble on pebble,
by measurement and all extrapolation
that give me a past and future
and mean I'll arch over the present.

When I come to the end of your finger I reach out
finding nothing, open to it, quivering,
with my little pod feet
swaying back and forth,
not able to make the leap,
and turn back on myself and hump back down
to the thin forest of hairs on your arm.

I am always in two places
the past and the future, never wholly present,
lost in repeated calculations
the stars taught me: a straight line
between two points is shortest,
and one and one equal one and one—
the moments dropping like pebbles in a pool.

I slide and fatten like the worm
of the Nile in the spring
leaving measurement where I pass
in mud and stone. The pyramid of Cheops
and all such monuments began
as I counted myself over and over along a stick.

I am of two minds moving out of sync—
when one's in action, the other's resting,
and so I never come to a conclusion
though we move in the same direction
by separate steps, by little omegas;
yet neither end comes ever to an end.

Though I am certain of nothing
except the arch I make for light to pass under
in a space I've measured again and again
in seconds and particles and waves,
when you put me on a green leaf
I blend in and am comforted
and forget for a while definition
in a wilderness of foliage, annihilating
all that's made to a green thought
that resolves the two halves of my brain
            until at last with the shimmering leaves
I flow upward.

Giant Panda

In the white mist of morning I find my place,
a square of the sun where I can balance

and chew the shoots, their green light in my mouth.
I sit, my footpads shiny, taking in the dim

sweet music of existence. On the mountain
when the enlightened one came holding the flower,

Kashya smiled. So it has ever been
as I move, myopic, from blossom to blossom.

I am the bear who sees your original face
a hundred years before you were born.

I sit, the world circling about me,
holding the secret between tongue and palate,

the sweetness of nothing, above which
the mind shimmers like a forest of silks.

for Ihab and Sally Hassan

Rabbit

They shall not hurt nor destroy
in all my holy mountain.
                    —*Isaiah 9:11*

I have learned much from the vegetable kingdom:
dandelions quivering in the wind, ready to explode,
milkweed that alights but does not stay.
I crouch under the peony, ears alert,
ready to leap, my scut bobbing
toward the hole dogs haven't found for years.

Like the plants, I listen underground
and store life there. In the vagaries up here
dew glitters on the grass for a moment,
clouds shift, and the dog lunges
from the lilac. So, swift and nervous,
I gather what I need—a trespasser
in what resembles paradise (a place
I dream of in my burrow, chewing on sweet root,
a place to trust one's belly to the sun,
in clover, where fox and hound nibble grass).

That is why now, out here, my eyes are round
staring with misgiving
at an air that moves treacherously,
where wind, rain, and sun are never still.

One night I dreamed of the moon,
saw her eye as bright and round
as my own, until I was drawn to her,
floated up to her like a milkweed
until I was lost in her vast circle.
In that light I saw all the rabbits
that had come or were to come—all silver—

except I could see through them. Yet each was distinct—
each with the others dancing slowly
on shining grass as they moved in a circle.
And as each left its place, another
filled it, till the first returned.
Then I heard the rabbit feet
beat on the moon, drum on her pale brass
until the distant vibration grew
and shook the earth, the whole ringing like a gong.
Doors and windows fell open in all the houses
and cities swayed while people ran to and fro
and the great grass-eating machines turned over
and fell to pieces and dogs howled
and crept back into their lairs.

Then the moon came down all silver
with ears like rays of light
and stepped into each pool, lake, and ocean
and swam there dazzling, all the while singing
of a beautiful absence of tearing and rending
among all creatures, of a peace which
surrounded each leaf like ivory fingers of moonlight.
Then she rose from the water and I could not look,
but put my paws over my eyes.
                                   And so I woke
in the dark burrow, damp, with the roots around me breathing.
It seemed I could hear the earthworms faintly singing
and the tooth of the grub celebrating in its darkness
and the roots of trees yearning down into the soil
like great mouths sucking everything to the heavens.
The smell of the earth around me was sweet.
Each crumb of it seemed a blessed thing,
each a world, a mystery, and a delight,
and, like stars flung across the sky,
each grain shone in its own light of being, each eternal
as this moment is eternal—all its sides pushed out
to infinity. Yes, even in this narrow burrow,
this small darkness, the secret glory,

all of it, entire—I cannot say how. And so I moved
up the tunnel, delicately treading on so much of worth,
and into the sun, which was music ringing from the green grass.

So I was there, and not there, I was with all things,
somehow the whole earth holding me and all things.
All fear was gone, the sense of being shut
in this quivering hide was gone: I was outside.
Rather, all these things were, and I not opposed to them—
not opposite, not alone, but within that secret music
faintly swelling from each blade of grass
in a green flame to the heavens, while the fragrance of clover
rose as a symphony, a fountain of color;
and I breathed it in and gave it out, and it was good,
there, before my burrow. So I lifted my legs and danced,
beating the earth, drumming it, solemnly dancing.
telling this to my kind and to all creatures.

Tiger

Tyger, Tyger, burning bright
                    —Blake

Like these shadows
I flow in and out of myself.
In a stand of bamboo, I am invisible
until my mouth flashes a rose
and another lies under my claws.

In the green shade I flow with ambiguities.
The birds above debate my arrival
until I take shape at the center,
absolutely necessary, giving form
to the redundancy of leaves,
to the panicked circuses of monkeys.

My voice, a low engine turning over,
guttering, has a certain resonance,
vibrates through every root, climbs through
the cilia of insect-eating plants,
travels along the vines
and through the toppling kingdom of the ant.

I drag my victim from the waterhole—
the cow, the zebra, the wildebeest—
and feast among my retinue, who boast
and chatter of my deeds at a respectful distance.
I am regal and lazy in my eating,
tolerant, when full, of those paying court,

hyena, jackal, and other politicians,
each suing for bones—his own and the other's—
while I perform my ablutions in public
like Louis XIV, no least fretting or cleansing

of my fur beneath the scruple of each eye.
You might say it is my finishing school—
not the least thing lost on those around me
of how they should behave toward one another.
You might say my feasting establishes order
that ripples out in circles

to the least and frailest link in my kingdom.
Even the table I lay is splendid
and instructive—glistering, colorful,
spread out in the sun—
creating symmetry, perfection, a hush
that follows on my velvet tread.

Spider

ZZ. The fly is at the sill. *ZZ ZZ.*
I am silent, riding the center
of my web, the intricacy of my thought
spelled out like the stars and the bonds between them.
ZZ ZZ ZZ.
My feet make no noise as I dance to the edge

of my galaxy, this gossamer star-net that catches
the gray light filtering through the window.
Here at the edge of the void through which I
extend myself, I listen to the fat
stumbler, him of the single idea
that the glass will suddenly dissolve, this one

who crawls upward on gluey feet and flails
stubby wings until he plummets, his eyes
rotating, twin red turrets. He tries and sputters,
tries and fails again. Satisfied,
I return to the tensile center, all my wits
sharpened to wait. For have I not written

out my thoughts to the gods?—I, who fell
from heaven on a single strand,
unraveling myself, and found this eminence
to attach to—and then that—and that—
in the void, in the whispering chaos,
and, groundless, swung myself through the night,

launched out on the rope of myself to meet
the other like an echo of myself,
trailing the strong cord of my being
in parallel dodecagonals until
the pattern of my soul was laid out. Then
the great square of day shone dim as the white

eye of the sun climbed up, and I saw
the beautiful design
of myself flex silver in all directions.
The small gnats fly to it in admiration
and sing, fascinated, as I weave them into it
and drink their song, my hunger slightly abated.

Now I wait for this sad, black-booted fellow,
this drab swashbuckler thick with the dust
of his fellows who failed before him—
this worn-out singer of song who turns
one eye backward in fear, one forward in desire,
who thinks there is a world outside the glass

of color and open spaces, grown tired of
my twilit world where things silver with thought
and dry up. Let him bluster and crawl!
Soon now, in his last careering search
for a way out of the dark he'll find my net,
a shimmer of moonlight sticking to his wings,

a deadly, impossible music that catches
him mid-air, a symphony that wraps
him round though he saw at it frantically
with his small violin until it silence him—
until he hangs, a note like the others
in this universal score I have composed:

my choral symphony, to which I'll offer up
his small soul in gratitude, that it might swell
larger, ever expanding in this darkness,
until he hangs, a shell as weightless
as if he'd vanished through the glass, transfigured
by the endless contemplation of my being

into my very self, a burned-out satellite,
a dead star. Meanwhile I wait
all night at the center
filled with a sweet surfeit of being,
sensitive to each wave and vibration
along its radii, listening for news
of life stirring at the far-flung edges.

One Word More (Spider)

Free me from
this web of words
in which I wrap
each passing fly

to eat and spin
into more web
until the corner's
one gray film

where deaf, blind,
and swollen, I
wait to be swept
into the sky.

Still More (BEE)

Let me not feed
on the honeycomb
of words,

but where they fall away,
on the wordless honey
of the Word.

Llama

In my end is my beginning.
—T. S. Eliot

I hold my head up, surprised by a white peak
you are at the wrong altitude to see.
My body floats in a graceful rhythm under it
but my head always maintains its simple poise.
I am the soft white of wool and yet inside
burns the impossible white of sun
on a distant snowfield no one has ascended
except my ancestor from Macchu Picchu,
a scapegoat, a messenger, an aspiration
the ancient Incas unfurled
to the severe deity of snow:
a banner, a dignity, a throne, a power.

Should you be lucky enough to ride my back
on a saddle of many-colored wools,
do not engage me in idle conversation.
Note how each hoof picks an invisible home
on the vertical rocks. All you can do is hug
the moving question-mark of my neck
as we pass over stark canyons
on bridges of snow, clouds
floating halfway down, the bells
on my harness accompanying us like birds.

No need to tether me at night, and at dawn
do not approach me directly or look in my eye
for I spit with notorious accuracy,
an unsavory comment on your indelicacy.

Notice how we have wound about these peaks,
how the trail has disappeared many times,
stone crosses marking the unexpected descents,
the thinning ether,
the great gods that burn at night above us
muttering and thundering in their sleep.
The streams merely gurgle now or fall like mists
across the vastness.

Your fingers turn blue outside of the serape.
You talk in your sleep of your lover, oxygen.
I listen with the silver ear of the moon all night
and bend to breathe a little warmth on your face.

When we reach the ice palace, the great snow field,
the flashing caves where the rainbow hums
in the green wall and meet the naked one
warmed by his own meditation, clothed
in the moss of starry speculations, he'll open
to you the first step, impossible yet simple,
of the journey you think you have completed
but which, in fact, you are only now beginning.

Nightcrawler

What I love I take whole into my mouth
and pass through it as it passes through me.
It is dark and wet and made of everything that has ever been.

I am blind and buried in it, yet it goes on
forever, in one silent mouthing, an endless aria.
I drink it in, and weep it, sliding moistly through it,

loosening it, even as it welcomes me, bringing the sky
down into it. I push, then drag
my whole self like a long afterthought,

writing a strange line looping in mystery,
now and then following the spoor of the others
through tunnels smooth with sorrow toward the light.

In the dark, broken by faint wormholes of light,
when the cool dew settles on us in the air,
we slide out into the naked element,

and find each other, wrap around the other
tightly. In that moment, anchored
to the ground and to each other in the heavens,

we are positive and negative poles,
electricity from earth to sky and back,
having the long speechless speech all flesh desires,

vulnerable as all flesh, no bone or beak to shield us,
blind, a naked want that has finally joined another
to a fullness, to a moment of no-time,

when all the echoes shaking the ground return in one sweet
                                                vibration
as if the earth itself would leap up and take form,
as if all life that has passed through us

would stand together and tremble into shape,
and stone itself, the rock keeping mute its secret,
would finally confess light, light,

and begin a slow and luminous dance of forms.

Lobo

When it is cold,
when the air cracks like a hundred-year-old tree,
when there is the thinnest nothing,
and the lake is clear and hard as the moon,
I come forth and sniff the air,
my fur around me sleek as thought.
I scent and scent and then
give the moon back to the moon in one long O,
give the ice to the moon and the yawning lake
and the stiff black fur of the trees,
and my O fills the sky
till the others come,
low, loping, yittering and yelling back,
lashing the air with their quick tongues
like a mob coming toward the palace,
like the tongues of a million unmarked graves,
like ten-thousand sirens in a thousand cities,
the gray, the silver, and the white with black foot.
We sit in council,
chasing the moon on its way,
supporting the sky, rounding out its hollow,
and our music is murder over the hills,
cold tongues on your back,
the sharp tooth at your throat,
and slaver glittering over your stiff eyes.
You, lying in the hollow,
you, turning in the cold bed, afraid to drop
down into the black lair of sleep
with its ten-hundred-million pleading mouths
and its insistent hungers,
you, before whom the electric eye flickers in the dark,
shrinks to a pinpoint, and goes out
after dropping at your feet a hundred corpses
from a dozen different countries,

each with a story, each with a vision
at which you can only stare without speaking
as they stalk you on lupine foot.

Evening Wolves

fiercer than evening wolves
                    —Hab. 1:8

Round and round they go on about nothing,
on the platinum compact disk of the moon,
the wolves. Their howls revolve about
the nothing that's eaten your life to its skin
even as it eats the moon to a thin rind.
Each revolution of the sound has a silvery
quaver, a light dip and resolution,
a tremolo, like recordings from the twenties
of voices sheer and faded as old silk.

Listen, the siren starts up again and circles
in its long ascent and decline about the rim,
its aria of desire and desolation,
a litany of memory and loss
and regret settled into like this broken chair
on a winter evening while the last light falls
unravelled by two flies at the window.
Cooling, they creep and stumble on the sill.

The wolves leave despair like a silver needle singing
in the blood, a fear of the blankness of snow,
of the hot slaver of hunger at your throat,
and the red eyes weaving a knot around you
while the fire gutters and you hear no answer
but a murderous vibration among the trees.

Worse still would be the absence of this fear,
locked in this cabin with yourself and the moon,
worse for the head lifted in ululation
to make no sound at all but a dry static,
the O of the empty mouth yawning, the vacant

syllable of the moon fading to a white silence—
no dark accusatory, no gathering of angels,
no judgment of teeth like a necklace of knives,
no unyielding jaws locked to your throat.
The last pain is the absence of all pain.

Just two winter flies, a jot and a tittle,
as the muffled clock beats against the silence
in the empty room, a jot and a tittle
against solid glass
through which you might make a run for the river,
risking the swift analysis of teeth
cleaving sinew from joint.

Better to be driven by the pack
through the trees toward the overwhelming sound of water
and, desperate, pitch yourself beyond yourself
over the cliff into the cataract,
into the thrash and thunder of Niagara—
risk drowning and a quick oblivion that at last
you might rise again, broken and absolved.

Rat

Peering warily over his moustaches,
with a dozen children to feed,
he pauses where he's pulled himself from the drainpipe,
his stare steady but not rude.
It says, his frank beast-like gaze,
that your house is likewise his,
that *mine* and *yours* are an elaborate game you play
as soon as you lay down a threshold.
In a twitch he's gone under the bush and you worry
about foundation holes you forgot to plug.

He is not inconsiderate or impolite.
He simply goes with the grace he's been given
and replicates his kind.
There, and there, they move like night,
faster than moths or oxidation.
At midnight you hear him rattle broken glass
in the dark rafters over your head
while the cat crouches, waiting.

He is neither obtrusive nor violent, this intruder,
and you may forget you've ever met him.
But one day when you've forgotten even more,
he'll gingerly carry away
what no longer troubles your memory:
even those little matters of dress
he excavates for, after a seemly time.
His tooth will not wake you, monotonous, insistent
as a clock for which you have no use.
You'll be alone when he carries off bits of your shoe
or bow-tie, watchband or silk pocket,
and, solemnly, I swear you'll not protest
when he carries off the ankle-bone

from which the burden of responsibility has been lifted,
until everything you have is his.

Look on him kindly, for at last
he'll carry you to a freedom beyond yourself,
out of the box you have built all your life,
to a sweet disorder in the dust.
There you may rise, sift, and riffle,
dissipate in the wind,
until you are part of everything
you didn't pay attention to while alive.

He will help you find what you talked about
and thought you cherished
until the sun shines through all your spaces
and you bless the water with your absence
and the air is your plain thought—
until all *mine* is *yours,* and *yours* is *mine*
and the words nothing.
                    Meanwhile
look on him kindly,
this ambassador from the Other—
adversary, beneficiary, brother.

A Lady Who Lov'd a Swine

I'll build thee a silver stye,
Honey, quoth she,
And in it thou shall lye:
Hoogh, quoth he.
    —*Nursery Rhyme*

It was those little teeth she loved most
showing at breakfast, the road-mapped
eyes over the shaking *O* of coffee,
the snuffling and snorting behind the paper,

as if his anger built a factory
behind a paper scaffold, a plant
to electrify her kitchen, made a place
of scorched toast, a Red Sea of counters

drained flat when he left. The ticking
fly-leg in the clock stamped each second.
She'd sit in the elastic mouth
of the armchair, rubbing a purple bruise

he'd given her last night—corsage
aching with color, drunkard's lovebite—
while the air waltzed with dust
and pain roosted in her nest of hair.

The brisk *chnnk* of mail in the box
would send her to the door, opening which
she'd let in the sun in its pert
gossipy way to enquire,

How could she stand living with the brute?
Didn't her face need re-upholstering?
She hugged the insult back to bed
like a hotwater bottle.

In the March afternoon she'd try to dig
up bird cries buried in the yard,
something muffled the sun might coax loose,
all the while listening for his shadow

and booming demand for a drink, his beery cheek
sanding her neck as he squashed her to him
tilting toward the icebox and boozy dreams
of swilling all night with the squealing girls.

And she would droop willingly and listen to the ice
ring music, ring money, under a a porcine stare
puerile and crafty—*Dearest, dearest piggy*
of her heart, rooting hot, stamping at the rails,
rummaging the husks of her endless love!

Ego

has thrust his nose under every board,
smelt out every wild carrot and white grub,
stucco'd the dirt with his tracks from side
to side, rubbed smooth the corner
posts, left his pink, red-bristled hide
on every barb of five strands of wire;

chewed the bark from the one scrub pine
that pitches a ghost of shade at noon,
bangs incessantly the metal trough-lid
at off-hours, chuffs down the white meal,
raising a cloud around his ears, and cleans
each cob with the nicety of a Pharisee,

tooth for tooth, squeezing contentedly
his small bagpipe voice as he mashes
corn with a slobbery leer and leaves
turds like cannonballs across a battlefield.
Meanwhile his little pink eye is
periscoped on the main chance—

the gate ajar, the slipped board,
the stray ducky that flusters through the wire—
saliva hanging from his mouth like a crown jewel.
His jowls shake with mirth under the smile
that made a killing on the market, won the fifth caucus,
took the city against all odds.

No wonder we shake at the thought of his getting out
of his square patch, electrify the wire,
(At night we hear him thump his dreams
on the corrugated tin hut and shudder,
the single naked bulb in there burning
through our sleep like his eye!),

take special dietary precautions against
his perpetual rut, except the March day
we drag the yearling sow to him
through mud up to his hocks. From that handseling
comes the fat litter—the white one for the Fair,
the spotted black to be slaughtered in November.

We don't show him to the neighbors, though in June,
framed by clover and bees stringing out the sun, he is
quite grand, an enormous blimp supporting
intelligent waggish ears, regally lidded eyes and
a pink glistening snout
ready to shove up the privates of the world.

Hog Heaven

In some dim sense he sees
it is already here,
the field of delicate corn, the glittering
wallow where each rolls free
of the hill of flesh, of the jawless appetite
that inhales a world of garbage and shrieks *More*
(as if the skin didn't have a decent limit)—
that tries to thrust himself upon himself
until all flesh balloons to one vast Pig
on which he is the smile, satisfied.

Dozing on the warm cement he dreams
that the sun, puzzled, pauses in the heavens,
that *First one at the trough for swill*
and *Furthest from the draft at night*
are not enough,
that the sun-warmed fly, who now forgets to bite,
buzzes another tongue, and the lifting wind
sneaks glittering through the goldenrod
to whisper something else into his ear
before the whistle blows, *It's time for slops*.

Like straw such dreams trouble the water's surface—
the pig's persistent business of stuffing, rutting
and grunting to his fellows his narrow will—
until the box pulls up and the ham-faced farmer
with hands like shovels and two sly-footed dogs,
directs him into terror's empty room
over an engine mumbling and shaking like a fly.
Too late—he cannot think for the squealing mob,
hunger, cold, and dust thick in his snout.

But after three days without water,
sensing the golden sacrifice of bacon,
the roast's crackling holocaust,
he rises, hilarious as helium
and, winged above the anonymous pen,
a winter gaiety glazing his eye,
a seraphic humor slimming his jowl,
foresees and forgives all:
the rotating jaws, the dreamless fat and muscle,
the bland pink hands which lift the plate for more.

Octopus

Like a child who cannot hold back
from exhibits that say, *Do not touch,*
I want to wrap around everything,
feel its configuration in my limbs,
in my mouth,
as I wander the museum of the ocean.
You might say I have an oral fixation
in the tactile school of underwater things,
but sensitive, transparent,
I dart away at the least rebuff.
You can see my soul in my head
swell red as a rainbow
with anger, with passion, while my eyes
beg you to hold still for a moment
while I approach you from eight different angles,
like a novelist
running over with ink in which to hide,
hoping to partake of your quintessence,
subjecting you to the necessary compression
—a friendly squeeze, you might say—
taking you to the very center,
where my mouth lurks, shy as a parrot's,
ready for intimate conversation,
each piece small as a word.

Have you seen me, slight and pastel,
spangled with sequins,
swim up like a ballerina,
jeté jeté jeté,
under a flounce of skirts?
At a party, have you seen me stare at you,
cold and marble from between chunks of squid
on a platter,
before you swallow me like an oyster

in the middle of a sentence and drink,
your mouth trailing smoke—
lost in the steam of your intellect?

SSSS, I retreat
behind a curtain of ink,
or come toward you
undulating like a maharishi
levitating,
my limbs a flying carpet
under the *OM* of my eyes,
large, shallow, mica-shiny,
keeping a miraculous stillness,
a kind of lotus position,
at the center of so much writhing,
my tentacles a small celebration,
silk pennants fluttering about me:
my oriental invitation
to a calm you can't resist
in my long and thoughtful embrace,
my light, manifold caresses
poring over you pore by pore,
studying every inch
with a touch and a glittering eye
during your gradual assimilation
and ultimate transfiguration
to this ink I squeeze out behind me.

Mussel

I am
tasting the ocean
one mouthful at a time.

It is a slow rumination,
a reading of incunabula
in my cloister

in this cell where light
fills me totally like an eye,
then washes away.

It is a sifting, sifting
as the animalcules make
a tiny crystalline circus.

I collect essences
while the Atlantic waits
for the Sea of Japan—

it is only a matter of time.
Meanwhile each raising of my shell
stirs all the waters of the earth.

The slow tides call me home
but I stay and savor
these identical moments

that pass and pass
in a still monochrome.
I have a single foot

and can make short journeys
out of this box,
its lid gleaming above me.

The myriads rush over me,
the small translucent beings
with their armature

and transparent tubes
swept by the slightest current,
heaped up in cities,

evaporated on a rock.
I close like night upon them.
They become my slow thought

rising toward that light which floats
over me in the dark,
spreading itself on the waters.

Soon I will be ready to leave.
When the light swallows me
part of me will hesitate,

hang back at the hinge,
a little bit of flesh revealing
the radiance of my absence.

Peeper (1)

I have been set aside, an ecstatic
among these pale green pillars.
All day I wait, my nose above water
while the great fire blinds and purifies
and the priests, hovering blue and red,
buzz and whine nearby,
until the fire dies and all things grow dark
in the low lapping noise along the shore.

Then tiny fires appear in the sky,
and a radiance, a blur; soon
at the moon's silver ray my chant begins.
Her belly swells with silent music
never-ending, unheard by the ear
that my feeble joy assaults all night
while she floats up and over the world,
round as this pond
that holds her as she holds it.
She sings of the pond,
of the fish that lurk like arrows of desire,
of a million trembling reeds,
and all that splash and flap around its edges:
the raccoon that washes what it steals,
the shadow that lowers its head to drink
and raises it, dripping, to stare.

She sings to the pond, which sings to her,
giving back her echo, her reflection,
while the little moon in my throat swells and erupts,
shaking the air with my news,
disturbing the waters under me
and reflected stars like a school of fry
while she slips down to the water,
quivering in a drop on this pad
and that one.

When I leap in —*plop*—
she divides to a hundred tadpoles of fire
swimming back to one—rocking to one—
and I am beside myself all night.

Silverfish

It lives in the damps of rejection,
  in the dark drain, feeding upon the effluvia
    of what we are, of what we've already been.

Everything comes down to this: we are its living—
  the fallen hair, the fingernail, the grease from a pore,
    used toothpaste, a detritus of whiskers and dead skin.

All this comes down and worries it into life,
  its body soft as lymph, a living expectoration,
    a glorified rheum. In the silent morning

when we least expect it, it is there
  on the gleaming white porcelain: the silver scales,
    the many feelers *busy busy*, so fast, it is

unnerving, causing a certain panic in us,
  a galvanic revulsion *(Will it reach us*
    before we reach it?), its body

translucent, indefinable, an electric jelly
  moving with beautiful sweeps of the feet
    like a sinuous trireme, delicate and indecent,

sexual and cleopatric. It moves for a moment
  in the light, while its silver flashes and slides,
    and part of us notices an elusive beauty,

an ingenious grace, in what has been cast off.
  As if tears and the invisibly falling dandruff,
    skin cells and eyelashes

returned with an alien and silken intelligence,
  as if chaos were always disintegrating into order,
    elastic and surprising,

as if every cell had a second chance
  to link and glitter and climb toward the light,
    feeling everything as if for the first time—

pausing stunned, stupefied with light.
  Before we, frightened by such possibilities,
    with a large wad of tissue come down on it,

and crush it until it is nothing
  but dampness and legs, an oily smear
    writing a broken Sanskrit on the paper,

a message we choose not to read
  before committing it to the water
    swirling blankly at our touch,

hoping that will take care of it,
  trying not to think of it—the dark
    from which it will rise again.

Slug

White, moist, orange,
I crawl up the cabbage leaf exposed,
too much like your most intimate parts
to be lovely, to be loved. I weep to the world,
my trail a long tear, defenseless
from its beaks and claws
except for my bitter aftertaste.
He who touches me shares my sorrow
and shudders to the innermost—my pale horns
reaching helpless into the future.
In plastic cups filled with beer
ringed like fortresses around your garden,
your lie of plenty,
we drown by the hundreds,
curled rigid in those amber depths,
so many parentheses surrounding nothing.
You do not understand nothing:
the nakedness to the sky,
the lack of one protective shelter,
the constant journey.
Millions of us wither in the margins
while food rots close by.
Nothing is a light that surrounds us
like the breath of God.

Caterpillar

I arrive slowly where I'm going,
in segments,

eating my way along in a compulsion
that strips the green ground under my feet.

I have doubled in size many times
but seem to be going nowhere. The leaves

tremble and hardly bear my weight.
I am tired of this constant consuming

and yearn for sleep, for darkness,
for a stillness within myself and in these legs

that jerk along at different tempos
until all my parts twist and bump together.

I know I can go where I have to,
but no longer know why. I have been

to the top and found only blank air,
unmitigated heat, and crawled back down

to a greener, cooler altitude. Here
my thoughts grow heavy with sleep.

Now I shall draw tightly
within myself and spin these lines,

a kind of silver-gray nothing
to hide the green world with,

weaving a stillness where I dream
of something stirring at the center,

that doesn't cumber itself with itself,
nor eat itself along a leaf at a time,

a thing lithe and alert
that feeds on light

and leaps upon the air
and fire, shudders upward to the fire.

Muskie

Eyes hoarding dull gold he lurks
at the bottom,
holding the lake steady
in water the color of bock beer.
He has aged for decades,
in season, out of season.

Above him motors unzip the sky all day
and zip it up again
as he lies under layers of water
turning the drowsy
silk of his fins, watching shapes
panic across his ceiling.

Light fades. The wind drops.
Shapes grow clearer
on the surface, except for a wavering
ghost of birches, the quick cipher
of waterbugs. A yellow lamp
gleams and dissolves.

Then, from under the dark
fallen tree he shoots
on a straight tack, seizing
the sputtering plug, diving
against the light,
shaking the first stars from his tail.

Hauled-in, black and silver,
blood mapping his throat,
chewing the air of a pitiless altitude,
he beats a tattoo
on the aluminum hull, listening
to the deep waters

grow still
more silver in a moon that climbs
finless, among the stars.

Grasshopper

Climbing up the stem toward the ripe
grain, he dreams about the green center

of the kernel while each leg winches
and cranes, pulling him higher.

A breeze comes and the sky wobbles,
the sun shaking a mighty *yes* or *no*,

but still he clings to the thin cable
until a shadow passes over and he

kicks free, flying toward the sun
on a parabola bending high

over the golden faces of the wheat
clustered on long stems.

He catches one, which bobs, shivers,
grows still. Again he starts to climb,

pausing only to make a thin music,
rubbing his hind legs together—

windharp, dulcimer—
in a field fat for harvest.

Together his kind scratch their hymn,
a thin sound the sun drinks up

as they wither in this late August.
At night the stars come out like cold

bright teeth to eat the world
while he goes low and creeping

until the sun spills its red light again.
Despite the random shadows

of crows crossing the field,
he rises toward the noon light,

rubbing his legs in praise, ready to leap
at a shadow's passing

beyond everything he knows.

Water Strider

He walks on water
with long, tensile legs
skates the surface of this element
leaving no ripple, no distorted clarity
never breaking the surface tension
quite at home in the sky
mirrored under him.

He is no philosopher
though you might think him one
where he moves like an artist's eyelash
delicate as a thought, a contact point
a synapsis
between water and sky.

The thought he embodies cannot be
translated into language
only experienced
in the languorous stroke
through oils
in the sky laying itself upon water.

From the side he is Fred Astaire
dancing on a mirror
making it look like air, as if air
and gravity never wed—
debonair, a gentleman
of equilibrious smile.

In the green and flittering shallows
a watery prism, he wavers
over the many-colored shadows, a kaleidoscope
turning the world in a dance
his shadow revolving
like a zodiac on the sand
beneath all suspended in the clear element.

He writes one word over and over
though no one will read it
before it vanishes: so clear, it is
transparent, his *mene mene*
that leaves the thing itself
before you think of it as *that*
before it is *that* and not *this*.

Though he writes his word over and over
he leaves no mark, not even a line like skywriting
to hang in the air an instant. Now
in the moment of his stroke are color and shape
a pattern light flashes around, a point
that vanishes and appears
to vanish again.

Daddy Long Legs

I am a circle. My perimeter moves
in any direction—up, down
sideways, forward. My center
is the center everywhere, for I gather
the world around me where I happen to be.
It is alarming how quickly I climb
your khaki pantleg, then scurry over
the grass you brush me to, climb up a tree
though I seem to have no head for direction,
hurrying and standing still at the same time.
One of me is as good as a thousand, for I
meet myself coming back through time,
matter and anti-matter,
monads and mirrors.
Though I move I am still here
and here and here and here,
my scurrying legs
the mere static of time
in the brilliance of being.

I appear to have no eyes, no ears,
no mouth. I am a single thought
surrounding itself, a singular idea,
an eye staring at the inside of the universe,
a pinpoint of light which holds within itself
the history of the Big Bang
and the revolving archangels of the Deity,
the Pleistocene and Waterloo
and the Grammy awards,
a singularity indeed
from which all flows and circles on itself.

I am brown
as a bun and a cushion button,
my legs thin as hairs.
Where I am, I hold all down
for a moment, then move on
invisible in the grass until
I am again crawling up your arm
as if desperate with a message,
as if to climb the air were no great feat
on invisible threads of light
to give some intelligence of earth to the sun.

A small Martian robot,
a space module, a moving camera,
a heat-measuring spectroscope
gathering the information of surfaces,
computing and sending it back
as I touch everything lightly,
measuring and radioing it
to a transcendent network—
my legs like the hair of Einstein
or the mad scientist's
or the movies where brains with beaks take over
and siphon everyone up until matter shrivels
and everything is just an empty sleeve
and earth spins away as a colossal thought
into the abyss of thought around it
and there is a vague hosannahing of antennae
and a chorus of small green blips
but gigantic thunders of imagination
and a pure gold dawn when matter reappears.

I am the careless aunt whose hair strays
over a face pregnant with black-eyed susans
and fresh currant-berries
with babies and poems that flew away in the garden
and a smile that dreams another world into being.
I am what didn't get tucked up when you were a child

and made a wonderful mess in the mud
under the cooking sun, the grass
bleeding into your elbows and knees
and the mud on your chin, the small pebbles
lined up and glittering in a row, your own sweet breath
as you moved things and saw them in a riot of newness.

I am a hot-cross bun on legs,
there for the eating, whose bones contain magic
like peyote
to alter the world. If you bite my center
you will never again be content with peripheries
or the long wastage of halls and the dim shores
of existence on the margin, but catch
the single reedy scratch of the sparrow
straight through your heart—
nor be tired from the hours of waiting and
the gray inconsequentials,
the violet of unfulfilled yearning,
and the fizz of desire,
the sad antics of the calculated moment
and the paper parapets of weeks and months,
but drop into the center
revolving slowly
pulling the world by you like a sea—
a strong swimmer
reaching out and pulling all things past,
lightly touching all surfaces,
taking everything and leaving it as it is,
rich with a word you cannot own.

Gnat

I am of no blessed consequence
in this vastness, and revolve
trying not to collide with my fellows
over the sun where it lays itself down
foursquare on the floor. The dust about me
swarms silver and gold in this light
streaming from the window
like notes of music in a visible symphony.
I dance, turn, and dance
with the dust in its glorious rotation,
moving up and down, divinely hilarious.
My wings are a thin film, growing
smoother and thinner in the air,
so nearly nothing that everything moves me.
My tears squeeze out smaller than mist.
Drowned in silence,
most can't hear my giddy laughter,
which joins hundreds in an arpeggio chorus,
deafening, but too subtle for your ear.
 Shall I, a gnat dancing in this light,
dare to be reverent? *

*The last two lines are adapted from Coventry Pat-
more's, "Shall I, a gnat which dances in Thy ray,
dare to be reverent?"*

Opossum

My one defense is stillness.
When you come
I am still, I finally am not there—
a vacancy in the air—
so blue, so empty, leaves
move through me and do not
touch my fur , nor my small eyes,
nor my tail innocent and pink as a worm.

I relax, am relaxed,
I am a fruit on this tree
that does the wind's slow samba.
I am an emblem of eternity. And you
turn, baffled by this somnolence,
to where feet skitter in the underbrush
and fear keeps all moving,
alert and on the sly.

But here in my dream
I ride the full arc of the branch's sway
a slow metronome.
Light rises, light falls
as I thoughtfully fold young leaves
into my mouth. Green,
their shadows flicker under the sun
in a green well, repeating
the infinite variety of things.

All goes too fast. I say,
Go slow, go slow—unhurried,
blink your eyes.

Upside down I climb,
suspended at each step,
feeling the heft of my body,
my toes digging into the bark.
Each step, each moment,
I am taken into a still world
of light, where all moves
without moving
where light pools within light,
each turning into the other,
where there are no walls, yet each
is itself and beyond itself forever.

But words dwindle like leaves
in a hard wind and I cry, *Breathe
slow, slow,*
breathe sweet and slow,
and ride this wind forever.

Hippopotamus

> *And quiring angels round him sing*
> *The praise of God, in loud hosannas.*
> *—T. S. Eliot, "The Hippopotamus"*

Hippopotamus to the Greek, *river-horse*, I move
still as an island, amid the reeds and mud,
my mouth, my smile, at the surface where silver drifts,
my nostrils twin caves for the river-smells, eyes
small and shrewd as a pig's. Between two worlds I dream
I am earth, the waters above, and the waters beneath.
I am the center: whenever the heat
blisters above me, I feel the river's cool nudge,
her dark veins below at my foot,
the sure currents feeling for the ocean.

I drift toward the shore. When I open my mouth,
it's like a ship's bow opening
to launch an invasion. But I am still
while the gooney bird picks about my mouth,
my teeth curved stumps stripped of bark,
my mouth a rose-plush box.
It closes and I submerge to breakfast underwater
on a pulpy and tuberous ton of plants.

When I resurface,
I jack myself from the water, my slick belly
pink and tender in places, walking forth
like a moon out of orbit, stiff and slow,
and roll over in the wallow while birds
skip and dance over what I churn up—priest of this mud,
my sacrament, which cakes me like a surplice.

Blessed by the mud, I blink absolution, benediction,
then trundle to the waters again, the bird
like an admiral steering me with his beak.
In the water I drift forward again,
steam escaping me in a great sigh of pleasure,
as I find the center of the river,
while egrets stalk and quiver in the heat
wavering over the plain in blue mirages
and clamor away in great flocks, always crying.

Mole

I am a prophet,
my eyes white and sealed.
I swim a long dark sea,
this tunnel,
pushing the dark aside
with hands like velvet gloves.
I am a slow swimmer.
In my stroke I dream
of stars that burn through this soil,
each a soft, white grub.
They come one at a time
to comfort me, but
they do not shine
except on my inner eye.
Yet I know the sky is coming
here where the air is bitter,
unbreathable as ammonia.

Once I thrust my nose above
and was blinded.
I felt pulled out of my skin,
splayed and waddled
mewling on the grass.
In that light
my ghost was written down beside me
and my shape thrown on a stone,
anatomized and judged.
I could feel the badger's lips
tighten in a laugh,
the white and black of his face
sort out my bones,
and the fox's nose moisten.
The great yellow eye
above swallowed me

and I hid
trembling under a leaf.
Then darkness poured down
over the earth
and I saw the stars
like small white roots
like bright flower-noses,
radiant pebbles
sharp as the teeth of voles,
each shining to the other
beyond the soil of night.

Again I entered the earth,
the long darkness of this tunnel
reaching on and on.
The beetle's scarab is good meat
on this wayfaring.
He is my pouch
and the mouse's thin bone my staff
while I head toward that room
where the mouth is sealed
with honey and wax.

For I know what this dark earth is,
that I hold in my mouth like a secret
while I dream and shovel
sleep aside from my nose
in this long chamber
and wait for the stars to fall
to their radiant kiln
and for one to come
through the fire
to touch my star-shaped nose.

Snail

In the dark backward and abysm of time
I make my home
lying here at its mouth
taking a little sun or reaching
into the slick grass

carrying the stone house of the past
with me, its heavy whorls and convolutions.
I am shy if a stranger comes
or night or danger
and reach back in, trying to hear

words from the holy cave of my birth,
what the shadows said on the flickering wall
in the light that teased me forward.
I listen to my own shell
to the ocean of becoming

to the flock of moons that led us to pasture
to the stars that foamed on the shore
tide after tide
drawing us up
the long climb on sensitive foot

over hard shingle
and the myriad shards of the others,
the white cliffs of bone.
Inside this smooth-lipped sarcophagus
that has ridden the centuries

I read glyphs on the walls
like the fossils of ferns
that have said something over and over
for a century of millions of years—
the curious bones of the mastodon

and ultrasaurus
that heaved up the sky
then lay down in a puzzle,
the trilobites that carried on wars
flashing coded messages

from under dark helmets
to die in a huddle
under the cliff.
I listen to each century,
its myriad events

that have gone unrecorded,
its dark hesitancies and reticences,
all those moments which crowded past
before they could be contemplated,
the questions answered and unanswered,

the cries in the night.
Here in my coiled horn
I crawl back into the rock
that leaked life in the beginning.
It is my oracle

through which the future speaks clearly
of what has gone before,
my conch, my ramshorn,
before which the walls shake and crumble
revealing the corpses in their mortar:

the uncomplicated green air
entering the lungs of a vireo
about to be shot by Audubon
or the terrible invisible bacilli
breeding in the blankets of Lord Amherst,

or the one who lived
looking from the second storey window
and recorded it on seraphs of paper.
(*Seraph/ saraph*, angel/serpent
turning together in the double helix).

My shell coils one way to life
and I coil the other way back into it—
matter and antimatter meeting in a Feynman diagram,
past and future the points of two cones
whirling into each other,

weaving consciousness, the brilliant
funklein of the present moment,
where all is possible, all is known,
burning nucleus, homunculus,
the utter penetralium of desire—

this cliff that totters above me,
this library I drag with me,
as I sign my path with tears
silver from my weeping foot,
this exclamation slurred on the rock,

this short word that dissolves
into the path of morning.

Seer

The returning honey bee performs a dance
to reveal to the others the exact
location of the source it has discovered.
In the dark hive, the other bees interpret
the dance by the air-currents from its wings.
                                        —nature film

Now imagine what would happen if he went down
again to take his former seat in the Cave.
                                        —Socrates

      Having found the gold treasure
of Atahualpa, the place of gold-dust one
can wade in up to the thighs, I do my dance,
my wings and legs showing precisely its
direction— the candle-tree's, the one
      whose gold cups spill over with heaven,

      whose gates of ivory blush
   purple, and whose every entrance is
an opening to a confessional where the soul
murmurs and grows drowsy with absolution,
  whose royal touch covers it with gold,
      there, in the flower's secret part.

      The others swarm around me in a fever.
   The sceptics urge their questions. There is an edge
of impatience, of anger even, as the zealots
ask me to try again and yet again
   to show precisely that point on the horizon
         where E l   D o r a d o   lies

119

beyond the bell of our ordinary sky,
the fields and orchards we labor in—to show
exactly where this tree is that is different,
whose blooms are storied lamps breathing,
like Ali Baba's, the seven perfumes
of Babylon—are throats that open

like the fabulous gold lake
of Montezuma, or the gates of pearl.
I am exhausted, and still I repeat the pattern
for those anxious to take off unerringly
to the source, eager to drone back,
bellies heavy with plunder

(so they imagine), freighted with 24-karat
until the cellars spill over, lucent with honey,
a sea of gold hoarded away in wax.
At such times I wonder: Could I live   this
dream for one eternal afternoon
while   light   shone

blazing in the sky before me
and feel myself melt into it one moment
to which there was no before or   after
but   only an IS of wings—
and   still come back to this dark cave
to fan its meaning on the wall

where the others feel nothing
but the current of air from my wings
and   understand my directions only
by blind intuition— come back, wings
frayed, legs feeble, to perform
this small dance over and over?

III. Ikons: The Two Adams

Adam's Dream

The Imagination may be compared to Adam's dream:
he awoke and found it truth. —Keats

He saw the garden spreading past the tree
he'd been warned to avoid (yet keep a special eye on).
He'd learned by scents, transported by the breeze,
myriads of roses and how, by hand, the scion

of one to graft on another—and what was edible:
whole families of legumes, grasses, roots,
melons, peaches, apples, pears. Incredible,
the variety of tastes just from the fruits!

But it wasn't enough. Even the breathing animals
with friendly grunt or sigh, silken warm side,
and large affectionate eye were not able
to speak. When he named them, none replied:

His words fell dead on the air—though he said
them everywhere, walking or running to each place:
to the mountain, which echoed back the sounds he made,
or the still pool, returning his own gaze.

But no one answered him until one night in a dream
he woke at hearing a soft voice speak his name.

Sheba

Bringing gold from Ophir and silk from Samarcand,
I came, your reputation having excelled
anyone's of whom I'd heard in any land,
and sharply questioned you till I was told

what man had never answered man or woman.
Until it seemed the hundred talents of gold
I'd brought with spices, apes and peacocks
were so much straw that, embarrassed, I took home.

Your wisdom turned the wavering sands to gold,
the face of heaven shone from each rock,
till I renounced my ivory throne, let go
the world that melts like sherbet in summer air

for a cave high in the mountains. Here, alone,
I pray for you trapped by your greatness there.

Ezekiel

Ezekiel saw the wheels within wheels.
His heart rose to his throat; a burning coal
purified both. The fear one usually feels
at such moments was gone. Transported, his soul

entered a quiet place, and while the creatures
moved without turning, he in his clear trance
noted their flight in detail, the particular features
of animal and angel moving in a dance

radiant as a rainbow. While there he heard
the awful message prophets usually bear,
before he saw in the valley of the bones
something more splendid than that which turned
in the heavens: dry bones grow whole and rise
and human flesh assume the immortal skies.

Annunciation

She didn't notice at first the air had changed.
She didn't, because she had no expectation
except the moment and what she was doing, absorbed
in it without the slightest reservation.

Things grew brighter, more distinct, themselves,
in a way beyond explaining. This was her home,
yet somehow things grew more homelike. Jars on the shelves
gleamed sharply: tomatoes, peaches, even the crumbs

on the table grew heavy with meaning and a sure repose
as if they were forever. When at last she saw
from the corner of her eye the gold fringe of his robe
she felt no fear, only a glad awe,

the Word already deep inside her as she replied
yes to that she'd chosen all her life.

What He Remembers

Both of us standing in the sour smell
of the alley, a head framed by orange light
jerked toward the stable.

where others slept in the shadows.
An old woman with a mouth round as a coin
laughed like a sheep

and offered us rags at a sheep's price.
But the steaming beasts helped warm the air
for the red face, small feet.

After things calmed down, we tried to sleep.
No luck though. Three field hands burst in
with a confused tale, talking all at once.

That spoiled our chance of any rest that night.

The Prodigal

She floated before him like a summer cloud,
pink and white through his sweat and then lay down
squealing, by her sucklings, a teat for each mouth.
The husks caught in his throat. If he'd only known
the pigs would have it better than he, he never . . .
He, ripe offal, stuck in the world's latrine!
—so he told himself over and over and over
and over again. With tears came a keen

ache in his chest. Next day he started home.
He tried to stop his thoughts, lethally busy,
but at night yearned for the slops and warmth of the barn,
the hogs' contented grunting and homely stink. Alone,
he knew he'd failed beyond all hope of mercy.
He didn't even see his father till wrapped in his arms.

Lazarus

Nothing tasted like a wafer on his tongue.
It wasn't new, he'd tasted it once before—
in the myriad of years before he was,
and *that* took no time at all, the *nothing* before

everything else.   As a boy he'd thought about it:
Why was there *anything* at all? The feeling
it led to was pleasant and dark, detached as if
he'd suddenly expanded to fill the ceiling.

And then, of course, the debts, the illness, the quarrels
between his sisters that drove him up the wall—
he'd left all these, thank God! Relief had swirled
through him with the fever until *nothing* was all.

But now this traveling magician with his meddling work
was drawing him back to his body—cold, stiff, and dark.

A Colt, the Foal of an Ass

Contemplating the dust he stands
in the direct unbearable noon, tethered
to the dead thorn. His long ears hang
down, twitch and revolve as a constant
small black cloud of flies
brassily land and bite and ascend. His hide
quivers at each bite and smoothes out
like this quake-tormented land,
while his bathrobe-tasseled tail larrups
and swats too late.
     His eyes, half-lidded
in the bleaching light, are fixed and still;
his plain, dull face perpendicular as a post,
his forelock hanging over it.
     He does not
turn toward the stranger who stands talking
with the two at the door. Only his muzzle,
soft as silk and still faintly pink,
twitches as his nostrils catch the foreign scent,
widen and lift his lip for half a second.
     Then
lazily he turns to look, eyes glazed, indifferent,
tugs at the harsh rope once, desists,
patient with donkey patience, already learning
the rough discipline that pulled him from the grass
and his mother's side.
     Now, without warning,
as if he feels a tremor underfoot,
some inaudible alarm from the world's core,
he bares his teeth and breaks the air with a sound
like a stone wrenched and crying from its center,

harsh and grating as a rusty hinge
on which the whole earth hangs.
                    Later
there is a moment with a crowd roaring
in surges long and hoarse as breakers crashing,
cool green branches to tread over the hot stones,
and flowers which offer a brief fragrance under hoof—
one moment of all those in the years that are to come
of fetching and hauling for masters bad and good,
when he does not mind what he is carrying,
when a sense of joy returns like the early smell
of grass when he first stood, unsteady in the field,
with a beast's dim sense of liberty.

Still, he cannot guess what he is carrying
and will not remember this moment in all the years
until he is worn out, lame,
until the hammer is brought down on his unsuspecting head,
his hooves melted to glue, his hide thrown to the crows—
when he shall return to this now, this always,
he continues to live in,
this moment of bearing the man,
a weight that is light and easy,
celebrated in a rough, ecstatic chorus,
toward his own fatal burden heavier than the world.

Judas

All along I was the only one who seemed to know
what the Man could do if he put his mind to it.
I'd seen him raise the dead, for God's sake, and control
the wind. Rome and her clackering legions would quit

Jerusalem tomorrow if he'd but say the word.
Or, if he wished it, thousands would die for him,
ecstatically falling upon the conqueror
with sticks and stones. So I waited for his least hint

of rebellion. But when he said he might choose
death, and how the Pharisees would see to that,
I couldn't believe him. Surely it was an elaborate ruse.
Surely at any armed threat he'd knock them flat!

He hinted as much to me, and I, conscious of the sin,
supped, betrayed, and kissed, that the battle might begin.

The Rock

Stars enough to break a net
And you could smell the new shoots
Groping after them. No moon:
That was my only hope.

After the other left we knew
Something was up. He led us
By that strange parting look.
Through night thick with trees.

We drifted in and out of sleep.
He kept coming around, silently
Accusing us it seemed. "Lie down,"
We murmured, "Lie down."

"Lie down?"—he laughed a little,
His shadow across the stars.
Occasionally a noise in the bushes
Tickled our fears.

I must have dozed off. Suddenly
Sleep in my eyes and fire,
Hooded shapes drawn up,
Then a flat voice: "He's ours."

Reflex!—his weary words—
The angry murmur of flames.
I tried to stay near. . . I wanted to see. . .
(Someone was taking down names.)

But tripped over my northern tongue—
I . . . I . . . not I!—
When that meddlesome bird
Broke open the bloody sky.

After "The Dream of the Rood" (ll. 1–23)

Lo, I will bare   the best of dreams,
what came to me   in the cold night
in the dread dark   after voices dwindled.
A torch of a tree   touched my dead eyes.
Looped with light   it kindled aloft
brightest of beams.   That whole beacon
glittered with gold;   hard gems studded,
enfolded the front.   Likewise five
spangled the shoulder-span.   Angels in awe beheld,
fair from the God-forge.   This was no foul gallows!
But there beheld Him   hosts of the hallowed,
men from earth's mold,   mirror of creation.
Lustrous the Lord's beam,   yet, I, lapped in sin,
overwhelmed in its wallow,   saw the whirling tree
now wax winsome   swathed in brightness,
garnished with gold   wield its wondrous rays.
At times I glimpsed   through the bright gold
woe of the wretched,   wounds where the blood
ran from the right side.   Wrung with sorrow,
forlorn at that fair withering,   I saw the fated wood
fuse shroud and bloom.   Now the wounds swelled
with the ganging blood,   now the gems crowned.

A Notable Failure

Holy Saturday

He never went abroad to broaden him
and though he learned to read, he did not write
anything worth saving. Once, at a whim,
he scribbled something they hadn't gotten right

in the sand and erased it. Few could know
whether to credit any of the vulgar rumors
surrounding his birth in a shed. There were low
whispers and a gap of thirty years.

Then more rumors trickled through the countryside
about the artisan's son turned wonderworker:
probably a charlatan—blasphemer to be sure. Wide-eyed,
some claimed he raised the dead (and healed *lepers!)*

before the Romans nailed him—as they nailed all such—
and the neighbors sniffed, "He didn't come to much!"

The Shroud

(at Torino)

the wild darkness of the Godhead.
—Jan van Ruysbroeck

One can read the linen like a battle map,
where the blood advanced, retreated, pooled.
Here creeks ran with it, there it blistered and dried.
Every detail is patiently recorded
as in monuments we wander through like tourists
vaguely uncomfortable, unwillingly involved.

Still his face rises above this moment,
at peace, like a bird carried above the battle,
bearing our days away on wings of light.
We find the love buried in these lips
waiting for the stone to be rolled—heavy clog
of the human heart, ballast of history.

Faint as an old tintype the image
hovers, masking an outrageous light
from the wild darkness of the Godhead—
the ravenous wings of Easter that will stoop
on death scurrying away like a spider,
shake the flowers out,
and tumble sparrows in a well of singing—

until at last we open and the garden going in
green robes seizes us with laughter
bright and terrible, blowing loose our hearts
like the Mary shaken from her cloud
to the enormous gaiety of light
and the whole spontaneous flesh
now and forever loved in its first being.

Thomas

The man was dead. I'd seen. And that was that.
I'd helped them bury him. The heart had stopped.
Later the women started in. Soon all were mad,
jabbering about seeing him, his wounds. They dropped

everything else and huddled to see a ghost
like the gentiles' squeaking wraiths and spooks.
At last I agreed to look but locked the door—no
tricks! Suddenly among them. . .I blinked and looked

twice—*He* was. "Thomas, put your finger here."
So I pressed the wounds—the hands, the side—
the flesh all torn pitifully. "My Lord, My God!"
Later He ate the fish and drank the wine

I handed him. I never took my eyes
off him, the living flesh, for which the starved heart cries.

The Epicure

It was a pleasant life: at night the temple girls,
occasionally, after lunch, the flute-playing boy.
A moderate life: poetry for the heart and prose
to temper the mind, though I found less and less joy
in it, that ineffable something in the humors
of youth. I was middle-aged. Then walking in the agora
I heard one speak of a strange god—surely just rumors—
but there was something in his eye, and I heard Pythagoras'

golden spheres turn for a second: the old joy returned.
Listening to him—scrawny, a head short—I hardly heard
his words for the music that lifted me: someone yearned
through it for me—a face? a light? a darkness? His words
at last trickled in, seeds through a sieve. Since then, this
life's meant cold night watches, fasts, tears . . . bliss.

Patmos

He was not in his dark cave; he was sun-bathing
on a winter's day, soaking up heat from a rock
when the sun advanced and split in two. In a ring
of light he saw a blazing figure—no great shock
for him, the bronzed feet, eye of fire,
John told his disciples. He was soon reassured
it was his old friend who had spoken in a whisper
when they last ate together. Then he heard

aloud the same glad promise: "If any one opens the door
I will come in to him and eat with him
and he with me"—John's habit at meals, and more
or less constantly throughout the day: in the dim
evening and morning to eat and be satisfied,
as in the blaze of noon and when the stars sang to his eyes.

IV. The Face of Light

Peonies

In June these
globes of white flame
swell, explosions so very
slow, we see in them absolute
fire at the center, stasis
of star's core,

or a fragile
moonglow distilled
ghostly in each alembic.
From their green ambush these
unearthly aliens assault
us with color

for a week
then gradually fade
into another dimension. As
Dante saw the stars in a glass,
a corolla of souls,
each reflecting

the other's light
and charity, so in these
low white spheres we contemplate
mirroring heavens: petals, tongues
stammering silent music from
one root of fire.

After Viewing the Bust of Nefertiti

for Ann

From the first day I saw her face
in this life, until this present sight,
my song has not ceased to follow her.
            —*Dante,* The Paradiso

Dear, you may not contest it: you
are beautiful as Nefertiti. True,
her nose, her smile, her swept-back eye
which gaze out at eternity
may not be *quite* as perfect, yet,
pity the helpless sculptor set
to render the impossible!
Likewise, if some reader will
reject my awkward verses' thesis
that you rival Akhnaten's princess,
the fault is mine: you are above
the clumsy measure of my love,
or anyone's. No matter how
skillful the hand that traced your brow,
the line would falter. You, my Love,
without her crown or make-up done
to please a pharaoh's humor, still
are beautiful—at the breakfast table,
delightfully disheveled, able
to vanquish all those others doomed
to be perpetually well-groomed.

Whether stooping among your flowers
or in more meditative hours,
the cup moving toward you at the rail,
a likeness of you will only fail
to reveal the *je ne sais quoi* that

grows where flesh leaves off—a light
Raphael released from paper, yet
beyond words startled into flight
by this poor pen—the shadow of One
who thought of you before the sun
was kindled, yet precisely here
and for this moment made you the dear
image of that beauty and grace
who loves us with a human face.

Spinning

The water is low and smells
  of fish and dark-brown weeds.
The boat gives under my step,

sliding out from the pier
  toward the center. Lily pads
hiss lightly against the bottom.

Taking my spinning rod
  and spoon I prepare to fish.
The oars swing aimlessly.

Two dragonflies hang in air
  mirroring each other and the bright
hackles in my box. The sky

turns a slow circle over me.
  Without a ripple, the lake,
a single eye gazing upward

at all that rests on the surface,
  takes to its heart, tree, cloud,
and the quick outlines of my boat.

For a moment the horizon
  focuses on this place
where I stretch out a thin line

and, thoughtless, draw it in,
  turning as the woods turn with me.
I toss out the silver spoon

over and over, not caring
  what it takes from the deep
root-colored water, knowing only

that a wavery image is written
  on the sky caught in the water
of a boat, a face, and an arm

casting something bright to the clouds
  and reeling in silver. Again
I fling it out, and again,

spinning from the center of the world.

The Gift

He lands in the elm, a shape of darkness
that casts no shadow in this milky light.
He stares at me and calls out once

to the rest, who leap into the wind and swirl,
black confetti against the clouds. Still
he hunches feathers up, pecks at a wing,

and stares again, until I move one finger and—
he's off, his claxon sounding over the field
far into the woods, wild and rude,

again and again, fading at last to silence,
leaving behind a perfect solitude.

Haiku 1

Logs cut,
stacked in rows:
winter dreams.

In the squirrel-proof feeder
a fat red one
sleeps.

Fingers cold,
the crow's cry
colder.

The cat surprises
himself in the mirror:
whose paw?

Power Out

Rain on roof,
candle in mirror,
cats in bed.

Inside the Outer Kingdom of the Khan

1. *The Dream*

At home the year turns slowly on its axis.
July groans from the heat; humid air
shimmers under a burning sky,

the sun's red ingot throbbing as it rises.
Trees release faint steaming ghosts
that twist, unravelling from their leaves.

He gives to each a shape where it climbs
above the cherries, staggering red
with fruit over the unmown hay:

paladins of summer, seraglios of clouds
with necks like marble towers, while he hears
a tinkling sea-blown music through the haze.

2. *The Journey*

Amulets, anklets, floating mousseleine
burn in his eye with sweat. A dry cinch
rots and snaps. The resentful beast

having chewed the cud of anger
destroys the offered fez. Now nothing
hangs in the baked sky but a bird

on wings like ashes in an updraft,
foil for the ego that would find
nothing but itself cloud-hung with ease

among cushions and perfumed servants
where the prayer wheel wanders among mountain bells.

3. *The Desert*

In the acid moonlight, the cold spell,
the drifting dune that gives beneath the foot,
the white waste where the hyena's laugh

comforts, he scans the illegible map:
stars pinpoint his rigorous dreams,
the Lion, the Hunter with his club,

the Twins of ego, alter-ego, the Fish
whose death is a shambles, and the Virgin
whose lamp irradiates the skeleton.

In this hard light, he sees the jackal's bones,
sharp teeth, and snout, the dark declivities
shadowing sight and ravin. Gone, these

fill with the minute trickle of the sand.
Old shadow-face, crouched in the desert sky,
features shrinking with the air

that eats his skin, watches the tides
of desire, projects his shape
against the barren surface of the rock.

4. *The Mountains*

In the far passes, all goods gone,
naked as that hermit of Tibet
whose breath clings to the ice walls of his cave,

saving his shrunken pulse in a moss of thought,
the traveler, having watched his last mule drop,
bells tinkling, down the avalanche,

turn over once and disappear,
despairs of his destination, takes a small
cloud drifting nowhere as his soul,

and at his wit's end makes a lucky guess
at a pass that twists and drops toward terraced slopes,
emerald with new shoots and fireflies
of lanterns marking here and there a hut.

5.   *The Outer Kingdom*

Inside the outer kingdom of the Khan
glimmer the inner kingdoms; a golden passport
opens each gate. The inner surround

the ever more interior, elusive
penetralia: a shimmer of kimonos, jade,
lapis, and the solitary bell.

A flute or drum now shapes the grove.
where paths broaden. The bridges wax ornate
with teak, ivory, and peacocks screaming

at apes in scarlet jackets. There is no end,
one within the other. He used to dream that
one day the great bronze doors with dragons,

each grasping half a world, would open,
the gong sound, and there at last,
prostrate, he'd slowly lift his head

to follow the golden incense up. . . Instead,
light of step, he wanders mountain, terrace,
valley, in and out—his camels loose

beyond the flickering palms. He, drunk on air,
the horizon toppling all things to his eye,
follows the elusive flute-note in his heart.

In a Farmhouse Near Porlock

In the summer of the year 1797, the author,
then in ill health, had retired to a lonely
farmhouse between Porlock and Linton . . .
   —*Coleridge's Introduction to "Kubla Khan"*

At home in her kitchen wife Sara grieves:
The tiles are unmended, the shoe money gone.
When she poured boiling milk on that abstracted form,
It had smiled and written a three-shilling poem.*

In a farmhouse near Porlock Coleridge sleeps
As the red moon licks itself to a ball.
A Collector from Porlock knocks loud through the hall:
Is anyone here, anybody at all?

By a farmhouse near Porlock a frayed moon sings
Like the bitter half of a wedding ring.
Huge blocks of night beat on the wall
And a tree shakes the green pulse of a star:
Nobody here, nobody at all!

In a farmhouse near Porlock sun and moon walk
Like red and silvery crabs on the sand,
Cold hand in hot where the heavens crack white,
And a head splits wide at the edge of a voice:
Is anyone, anyone here at all?

And there in the midst of the whirligig
Light put its stick and broke the string,
Night hooted by on its rickety rails,
The garden sprung, the day shook free,

All space snaked by and a mind floated blithe
As a bubble on a column of breath,
The lion rolled out his red-carpeted tongue,
Lambs leaped in the green fields of his breath.

Then the fist fell like a cindered star.
The door licked dry lips, the lid snapped down.
A Man a Man a Man from the Town!—
A shoestring was broken, the fire out—
"Here I am! Lord! Here I am!"
And Coleridge went out.

for J. Robert Barth

*An earlier poem, "This Lime-Tree Bower My Prison,"
Prison," was written after the recounted accident which
prevented Coleridge from going on a walk with
William and Dorothy Wordsworth and Charles Lamb.*

Connection

Lying on the edge of the boat,
watching my face in the water
fall apart and reassemble
in the long, graded light,
trailing one hand and my plug,
its last hook skimming the surface,

I watch the reflected clouds
blow through me while the birches
sway along the shore,
twisting shapes white and green,
and so don't see the dark
shadow under me rise,

lunge at the bait and vanish
as bubbles at the surface
spin on the eddy. I am
awake too late to his presence,
straighten and toss the lure
in a high arc to where he must be.

With a feverish sputter
the yellow plug flashes in the sun,
raises a commotion. Yet
I know all this is an act
of false hope and adrenalin,
a charade fishermen act out

after the moment is past.
He will not come back now
to me, stiff, intent.
Later under a cloudy moon,
perhaps—while I watch my shadow
climb and sink on the water,

listen to the thirsty whine
of mosquitoes gathering in hordes,
and sweat, glued to the thwart,
half-asleep from the boat's slight rocking
as it floats by inches to shore
over wavering black pines—

will his lightning strike my thumb
from the reel and the lake come alive
under the tilting boat.
Only then will I know,
while the dark mouth struggles with my line,
that for once I have really connected

(at the moment I didn't care,
drifting light as a feather)
with the waters under the earth.

Traherne

The corn was orient and immortal wheat, which never
should be reaped, nor was ever sown. I thought it
had stood from everlasting to everlasting. The dust
and stones of the street were as precious as gold;
the gates were at first the end of the world.

Centuries of Meditations—Thomas Traherne, 1636–1674

1

In God's green camp you sit in a silk tent,
flowers springing under your feet, intent upon
marigolds, goldenrod—sweet ragweed—
Ferdinand forgetful of the fly
which shakes the air with its small news of war.
The ramparts of the camp unwatched, you think:

Let Charles the Martyre go and Cromwell come,
turning his ear to horn inside the coach
while George Fox running beside it shouts for peace—
still at the still point Thy Kingdom comes.

We marvel how an angel like you came—
when precious stones were smoothed for every sling
that flickered at Goliath in the clouds—
to gather ordinary stones from the road
and wash them till they shone in a sluice of light.

2

The smallest grain of wheat would light the ground
like the sun or perhaps the moon gorging
on the summer air—

each drop of dew,
a world lying spendthrift in the grass,
and the sky dreaming between wheel-ruts
an image of the soul.
                    In the best sense simple,
each word is a single drop in a still pool,
a leaf turned up by the barest stitch of wind,
accommodating as the edge of a lake and yet
resting at its own level.

        To read your prose we need a kind
of smoked glass. Each sentence flashes like gold
dredged from the sea's grave—the absolutely
real, from which we startle like fish
streaking to hide in a thick net of dreams.

                    3

Suppose a river, a drop of water, an apple, or a sand.
Suppose the object in the patina of being,
cushioned on the infinitude of God, a light shifting
like a rainbow on the lake's sandy bottom.

Here is the promised rest—a motion and a rest—
the soul, Ezekiel's wheel full of eyes,
wings unfurling candescent Beatrice
while red and white and green dancers shift their ground.

Suppose a curious and fair woman, like this one
tense with the lineaments of fire,
busy about the two infernal refugees
dragged from the pit.
                    The poet turns to his guide,
the film through which everything might be borne—
gone, nothing now but fire beating air.

Derelicts

The giraffes totter onwards, sweet derelicts of heaven.
They do not cry to each other, they have no voice,
their mouths are dumb on the pennybread of heaven.

One is an albino, walking lightning,
an incredible architectural nudity,
the legs and angles we would melt upward into,

the nude ascending a staircase cubed in four dimensions,
all legs and lovely neck like the girl we saw
at fourteen at the mixer in the blue taffeta

and were afraid to dance with,
she moved so slenderly
like air moving in air

a column of sky
the invisible stem of a cloud
that led up to the piled morning of her hair:

the girl who was silent
whose sweet head swayed from leaves to invisible leaves
as she browsed the heavens and we

boys, shoes polished, lurked in the men's room
with hair oil, comb, and the panicked heart
entangling itself the more it tried to escape.

Like a simple idea uniting earth and heaven,
a simple idea marrying stars to the earth,
another dimension we could be beamed up into,

the answer to a question we hardly dared ask,
like Shelley's smile that kindled the universe:
escalator to *that. . . that . . . that. . .*

New Year

The sky is so blue history has vanished.
Each pine stands unentangled in the sun,

knowing the freedom of light, a fringe of snow.
The white forest floor is clean and smooth.

The tracks of chipmunk, mouse, and vole
are tentative, a wandering text to read

with nose or eye, saying what was never said
before this instant—the sun sprung from Eden

like that red fruit before its skin was broken
and knowledge was an unread story, an aroma

on which the soul got drunk. Each footprint's
shadow is new upon the snow, a word

transfixing body and spirit, a light that
never was on sea or mountain, springing

somewhere from the mind's root. Bless now
these graceful figures, a 2, an *O*, an *O*,

a 5, and free us from all false beginnings
accumulated in the past so we can live

this moment as it is, a beginning
with a middle and an end,

that in itself contains all other moments.

In the Solar Room

Sitting in the sun behind the glass doors,
the snow like a brilliant floor of clouds in the garden,

I squint, look aside, knocking on the darkness,
the light pooling at my feet and rising

past my knees, belly, sternum, to my throat,
pausing, and at last, filling my head

like thick nectar, like a wild electron,
so fast it is in every place at once.

Resting there, feeling the presence grow
intimior, feeling the simplicity, the one—

the eye through which we see each other, the same
eye, as Eckhart said, a steady presence

never not here, never not there. I am ashamed
at what falls under the instant of forgetting,

when the one becomes two, two, the many things,
and I, like fractured light, a thousand shadows.

Rest

I enter this little poem to be
at peace for a moment within its fourteen lines
like fourteen bamboo stalks making a tiny
hut where the filtered light is cool and green

while I sit cross-legged in the center of a mat
and think of nothing—as the light outside
moves from left to right and then goes out
before I notice. A cat cries and a bird

drops one note in the darkness, then another
and at last a sweet third. It is so satisfying
I can't decide whether
I am finally waking up or dying

Whichever it is, when I leave I'll carry this poem
with me to rest in on the long way home.

Haiku 2

> *"a somewhat in no-wise"*
> —*the Blessed John Ruysbroeck*

An oar dips:
the moon wobbles,
sails on.

The rower stares,
moonlight dripping
from his oars.

My boat and I
float on our reflection,
erased by each wave.

A fisherman drifts
into the fog—
his pipe lingers.

The sun drops
behind clouds—
a conflagration of angels.

Wings

Raphael's wings are gold, an airy gold that thins
to transparency like sun falling on a wall
and yet are deep and wide as sun taking
a field full in the morning or
burning wheat in the eve-
ning. When he flies
away, they are a
streak of salmon or
carmine along the curve of
the sea, and where his feet touch
last, whitecaps rise to rollers and throw
themselves in ecstatic, bright h o s a n n a s
o v e r and over against the eroding s h o r e .

Mornings at Seven

1. Waking Up

Today the sky is
butter on my bread.
Before I woke, the sun
climbed the white clapboards

inch by inch. I came to,
threw out the night's trash
and tried too hard. But you
had been there all the time
in the rug's green fibers
saturated by sunlight,
holding me up.

I used to slouch down
to breakfast, counting
sixteen lead beads
on a string.

Now the hours are dandelions,
butterchins, peaches—
I hear the stones plop in the garbage
as I open their golden mouths
one by one.

2. Finished

It is finished.
You have done
everything.
I am stunned.
There is nothing

left to do.
The house breathes
a sigh of relief.

All its joists, free
of years of support,
dissolve in the woods
to a rap of distant woodpeckers.

3. A Million Inches of Grass

Getting up today I found
a million inches of grassblade
grown overnight in my back yard.

Something had to be done.
With its usual whirr and thump
my mind pounced on the radio,

the endless static of desire.
I slouched to the bathroom, sick
of the mess of dead skin cells.

At the scratch of my razor, you
woke me to the snowfield of lather,
the red glittering drop on my chin.

4. Dandelions

A galaxy expanding
through green space.
My lawn's a shambles:
clay shows
in pocks and ruts.

My neighbors shave
theirs.   I
weak with laughter
among the violets
unleash a thousand roaring suns.

5. Sirius, The Dog Star

Dandelions explode
in the green heart of space.
Supernovae radio
static of a different music.

Between them violets lurk,
ionized purple gases,
nebulae that bend right
off the spectrum.

Among them the dog moves,
an unleashed constellation.
Black holes, white holes—
elusive quasars—

he takes them all in
a mind of pure smells,
reading news of the cosmos.
Again his pink tongue

slips out, trembling,
polishes his wet, black nose.

Easy Rider

Gold fills my fingertips.
My heart keeps
count behind and just

above the garage. Blue,
colloped by the harp-strung
locust, drowns my iris.

My stomach cruises
under the Pole's green ice.
Unknown to mankind

my left foot
passed through Arcturus
yesterday.

Love, love, easy rider,
put me back together but put
the world inside me now—

small lethal puzzle
of scuffed and intricate
beauty heart must hold to.

Half a Second

A movement like a shutter's
and I am outside the dark box—
the ship suddenly outside the bottle.

Instead of empty, everything is full.
There is no absence:
every sail luffs out, every rope sings.

There is no more to be said.
There never was,
but one goes on saying. It is

the hopeless addiction of the tongue
to an ecstasy of particulars:
the snap of young peas, the onion's bite,

the tomato's pulsing alarm
the lupine's lavender finial,
the white cat by the feeder

in a raptus of hummingbirds.
Not only this place, this time,
but all places, all time:

everywhere—nowhere.
It is freedom, it is laughter.
Closing the eyelids and raising them.
That white cloud hanging there forever.

Haiku 3

9 A.M.

Yellow flames flutter
about the feeder:
a Pentecost of finches.

Prophet

The crocus holds
in purple lips
a burning coal.

Stars

Thousands of years
we've not understood
what they say all night.

Brief Petition

O God
whose great ear
swallows me.

A Song of Praises

for the gray nudge of dawn at the window
for the chill that hangs around the bed and slips
   its cold tongue under the covers
for the cat who walks over my face purring murderously
for the warmth of the hip next to mine and sweet lethargy
for the cranking up of the will until it turns me out of bed
for the robe's caress along arm and neck
for the welcome of hot water, the dissolving of
   the night's stiff mask in the warm washcloth
for the light along the white porcelain sink
for the toothbrush's savory invasion of the tomb of the mouth
   and resurrection of the breath
for the warm lather and the clean scrape of the razor
   and the skin smooth and pink that emerges
for the steam of the shower, the apprehensive shiver and then
    its warm enfolding of the shoulders
    its falling on the head like grace
    its anointing of the whole body
    and the soap's smooth absolution
for the rough nap of the towel and its message to each skin cell
for the hairbrush's pulling and pulling
   waking the root of each hair
for the reassuring snap of elastic
for the hug of the belt that pulls all together

for the smell of coffee rising up the stairs announcing paradise
for the glass of golden juice in which light is condensed
   and the grapefruit's sweet flesh
for the incense of butter on toast
for the eggs like two peaks over which the sun rises
   and the jam for which the strawberries of summer have
   saved themselves

for the light whose long shaft lifts the kitchen
    into the realms of day
for Mozart elegantly measuring out the gazebos
    of heaven on the radio
and for her face for whom the kettle sings
    the coffee perks
and all the yellow birds in the wallpaper spread their wings.

Aubade

1

Then shall all the trees of the wood sing for joy
    while each leaf thrusts into the universe of air
and the light green haze of April rises like smoke
    sweet in the nostril. Let the mind fill the hemisphere
of day while the sun beats a million white wings.
    Let each yellow and red bud in the dew
blaze forth with a hundred suns while night
    picks up her gauze and vanishes over the hills.
Let the rabbit's eye shine while he drums the turf
    summoning his brethren;
the squirrels spiral down, their tails like clouds,
    to clatter among the woodsy rubble;
and the shrew shriek and hide herself under the root.

2

The cat stretches by the window and cries at the door;
    the dog yawns, then yelps at the rising sun
that will run all day till it drops in the west.
    The mattress creaks as the man rises to fix breakfast,
his back telling him he is—*ah!*—alive
    while the neighbor's car snorts and gulps air—
in an ascending whine.
    Children feel their way through cool porcelain bathrooms,
teenagers dream a world of shimmering electric presences
    and clothes rise from the dresser to glide across the skin,
the belt firmly encircles the waist
    and the tie mounts to prop the chin.

3

Yet, staring back from the bathroom mirror are
    the ghost of the office, the boss's purposeful smile,
fog of the night's dream, the nattering conscience,
    the gluttonous mortgage, the skin in love with gravity,
and the razor's unkind cut—awareness of
    what is done and undone—the thousand engines of
                                destruction
the cerebral cortex draws across its synapses
    toward the fragile sanctum of the present moment.
Let each ghost wither and vanish in sunlight,
    crisp to the nothing it is,
while a joyful procession dances along
    the myriad lightning pathways of the mind.

4

Tree and house are clear in this moment
    when light is given shape and each thing pauses,
itself—before the frame blurs, the attention fails
    and we fall into one or another distraction:
the horrors and banalities of the news, the half-typed letter,
    the mysteries of long division, the tumbled tower of blocks,
regret's heavy shadow or the usual obsession.
    Lord, in the bright vehicle of this moment,
descend to us and spread your golden tent
    that we might keep sweet breakfast together, your beard
                                dripping
honey as we ascend the dayspring of your eyes
    into an emptiness that is present, solid and real.

Not This, Not That

Are you the ragged yellow fields?
No, the grass, broken and happy.
Are you the air, damp and intimate?
No, the deer's flag, her hoof muffled in the swamp.
Are you the sun patiently peeling the clouds?
No, the star in the dawn's throat.
Are you the stones bearing me up on their safari?
No, the acorn's hat, where its thought grows sweet and whole.

I am all these, and yet none:
Not the red streams flooding the banks of cells.
nor the river hungry for the ocean
nor the crow's feather that dandles to the ground
nor the wind trafficking in perfume
nor the little pool holding a syllable of water.

Still, I am where the tongue presses the roof of the mouth,
in the crease of the closed hand,
in the foot hesitating on the stoop,
in the eye that draws its shape on the sky
and lingers, waiting for the face of light.

Voice of Many Waters

*To him that overcometh will I give to eat of the hidden manna,
and will give him a white stone, and in the stone a new name
written, which no man knoweth saving he that receiveth it.*

                                        —*Rev. 2:17*

The night is cluttered with stars.
    The drift of the earth
is dark, enormous
    bulking shoulder of the undersea whale
in the Atlantic's winking canyons.
    Trees wait
for the slow stain of day
    walking now over the water
west of England.

    I put two sticks on the fire
on the ghost of logs
    that fade into the red eye
drawing the circle of my campsite
    about which hang
my all-weather tent, glinting axe
    myself, like planets
inching the swarm of stars.

    Twelve o'clock:
The beast startles first with his foot
    broad as unbearable moon,
his leg the shank of stars
    his mane the black roar of space
turning to the white heart of fire
    in which begin to move
thick and uncertain
    the rivery shapes of trees

bending over water
  cradling a platinum light
running to gold
  and pebbles
each speckled with suns
  each turned and lapped by the water.

Green steals over me:
  I am swung in a net of leaves.
Birds wrap me tight in their songs:
  drunk with the trauma of flowers
I am and I hear a voice calling
  within the voices of water.
A shadow brightens the ground.
  A hand darkens all but itself.

Somewhere in the face of the trees
  a large clumsy beast is singing
the brood of pain and music
  played on the stops of the worlds
the flute of starlight and vacuum
  the unending theme of Abyss
and the trees are growing before me
  translating all to flowers.

Now the voice is within a white stone
  round in my hand like water
that speaks one word running through fingers
  to shred in my mouth like the moon.
Outside the sun is rising. Blue,
  the sky is blue
and the far forest neighing.

  I wake in the orange flower of my tent.

for Clyde Kilby

Rinsed with Gold, Endless, Walking the Fields

Let this day's air praise the Lord—
Rinsed with gold, endless, walking the fields,
Blue and bearing the clouds like censers,
Holding the sun like a single note
Running through all things, a *basso profundo*
Rousing the birds to an endless chorus.

Let the river throw itself down before him,
The rapids laugh and flash with his praise,
Let the lake tremble about its edges
And gather itself in one clear thought
To mirror the heavens and the reckless gulls
That swoop and rise on its glittering shores.

Let the lawn burn continually before him
A green flame, and the tree's shadow
Sweep over it like the baton of a conductor,
Let winds hug the housecorners and woodsmoke
Sweeten the world with her invisible dress,
Let the cricket wind his heartspring
And draw the night by like a child's toy.

Let the tree stand and thoughtfully consider
His presence as its leaves dip and row
The long sea of winds, as sun and moon
Unfurl and decline like contending flags.

Let blackbirds quick as knives praise the Lord,
Let the sparrow line the moon for her nest
And pick the early sun for her cherry,
Let her slide on the outgoing breath of evening,
Telling of raven and dove,
The quick flutters, homings to the green houses.

Let the worm climb a winding stair,
Let the mole offer no sad explanation
As he paddles aside the dark from his nose,
Let the dog tug on the leash of his bark,
The startled cat electrically hiss,
And the snake sign her name in the dust

In joy. For it is he who underlies
The rock from its liquid foundation,
The sharp contraries of the giddy atom,
The unimaginable curve of space,
Time pulling like a patient string,
And gravity, fiercest of natural loves.

At his laughter, splendor riddles the night,
Galaxies swarm from a secret hive,
Mountains split and crawl for aeons
To huddle again, and planets melt
In the last tantrum of a dying star.

At his least signal spring shifts
Its green patina over half the earth,
Deserts whisper themselves over cities,
Polar caps widen and wither like flowers.

In his stillness rock shifts, root probes,
The spider tenses her geometrical ego,
The larva dreams in the heart of the peachwood,
The child's pencil makes a shaky line,
The dog sighs and settles deeper,
And a smile takes hold like the feet of a bird.

Sit straight, let the air ride down your backbone,
Let your lungs unfold like a field of roses,
Your eyes hang the sun and moon between them,
Your hands weigh the sky in even balance,
Your tongue, swiftest of members, release a word
Spoken at conception to the sanctum of genes,
And each breath rise sinuous with praise.

Let your feet move to the rhythm of your pulse
(Your joints like pearls and rubies he has hidden),
And your hands float high on the tide of your feelings.
Now, shout from the stomach, hoarse with music,
Give gladness and joy back to the Lord,
Who, sly as a milkweed, takes root in your heart.